DOROTHY L. SAYERS

RECOGNITIONS

Dick Riley, General Editor

detective/suspense

Dorothy L. Sayers
By Dawson Gaillard

Raymond Chandler
By Jerry Speir

Ross Macdonald
By Jerry Speir

Sons of Sam Spade: The Private Eye Novel in the 1970s
By David Geherin

science fiction

Critical Encounters: Writers and Themes in Science Fiction
Dick Riley, Editor

Frank Herbert
By Timothy O'Reilly

Ray Bradbury
By Wayne L. Johnson

DOROTHY L. SAYERS

By Dawson Gaillard

Frederick Ungar Publishing Co. / New York

Library of Congress Cataloging in Publication Data

Gaillard, Dawson.
    Dorothy L. Sayers.

    Bibliography: p.
    Includes index.
    1.   Sayers, Dorothy Leigh, 1893–1957—Criticism
and interpretation.   I.   Title.
PR6037.A95Z67   823'.912   80-5344
ISBN 0-8044-2222-2
ISBN 0-8044-6169-4 (pbk.)

To my father, George P. Forman,
who rescued another critter

CONTENTS

PREFACE

In his introduction to a contemporary detective work, G. K. Chesterton described the relationship between author and reader as follows: "If it is the first rule of the writer of mystery stories to conceal the secret from the reader, it is the first duty of the critic to conceal it from the public. I will therefore put my hand upon my mouth." As a writer of detective fiction, Dorothy L. Sayers fulfilled her part of the bargain. Please be warned, however, that as a critic, I do not put my hand upon my mouth. In order to demonstrate relationships among Sayers's works, I often must tell on the criminal. To avoid premature knowledge about the plot, the reader is advised to read the work before reading my discussion.

The readers for whom this book is written should already know enough about Sayers to know her major characters—Peter Wimsey and his helper, Bunter—and at least one of their cases. My first reading of Sayers was *Gaudy Night*. Its dense texture and its social commentary about women and men intrigued me. I wanted to know the relationship between so erudite a novel as *Gaudy Night* and Sayers's other works. In tracing the relationship, I discovered a wonderfully disciplined, humorous, talented, and—sometimes—haughty woman.

Dorothy L. Sayers may be known to detective-fiction readers only for Peter Wimsey or to academicians only for her essays about Dante and her translation of his *Divine Comedy*. Because I was writing this book for the Recognitions series, I concentrated only on Sayers's detective fiction. Her other works are in the wings, however, and I hope that my study points the way to them. I also hope that my admiration for her as a writer manifests itself, particularly in the last chapter.

The first chapter presents a brief biography, including Sayers's membership in the Detection Club. The second chapter examines several of her short stories, concentrating mostly on those that feature Peter Wimsey and Montague Egg. Chapters 3 through 6 discuss Sayers's novels in chronological order, to show how she gradually improved her craft and fulfilled her goal to combine the detective novel and the novel of manners. In accomplishing this goal, she gradually found her voice, which she then used in her later work.

Sayers believed that unless one expresses an experience, one has not had the experience, but has only felt its effects (see "Towards a Christian Aesthetic" in *Unpopular Opinions*). As she wrote her detective stories, Dorothy L. Sayers was learning to express her experience of the years between two world wars.

Chapter 7 summarizes Sayers's aesthetic and social concerns. It was these concerns—so relevant to us today—that first attracted me in *Gaudy Night*. We live in times much like those described in that novel and in Sayers's essays, times when people resort to materialism in an effort to fill the vacuum of spiritual disillusionment. Her views are worth considering.

For the teacher of detective fiction, this book offers specific information about the genre. I quote primarily from contemporaries of Sayers and Sayers herself about the art of detection. For the reader interested in what came before Sayers's religious dramas, essays, and her translations, and for those interested in popular literature of the years between World War I and World War II, this study, I hope, will be illuminating.

Mechanics

Sources for material quoted within the text appear in the Notes section at the back of the book. Superscript numbers have been avoided in order to enhance reading ease. Quotes are identified by page number and a few relevant words.

Acknowledgments

When I began my research, Colleen B. Gilbert and Joe Christopher generously provided materials and advice. Jerry Clack of Loyola University read some of the early chapters. I can never repay the kindnesses of the staff of the Marion E. Wade Collection at Wheaton College: Dr. Clyde S. Kilby,

Curator, Barbara Hendershott, and Marj Mead. My thanks also go to Alzina Stone Dale for her advice and to Dave Lewshenia for his help when I was at Wheaton.

Without the Loyola library staff, I should not have acquired many materials; therefore, I thank Mark Flynn, Dennis Trombatore, and Pat Doran. I am especially grateful to Loyola University, which extended funds and time that made my research possible. I also gratefully acknowledge Helen Williams for typing the manuscript and Patsy Krause for general and consistent support, which meant more than she can know.

For any research on Dorothy L. Sayers, one can never overlook the valuable assistance of Colonel Ralph Clarke of the Dorothy L. Sayers Society, Roslyn House, Witham, Essex, England. And last, but never least, my appreciation goes to editors Dick Riley and Olivia Kelly Datené.

DOROTHY L. SAYERS

INTRODUCTION
The Essential Mysteriousness

Dorothy L. Sayers tells us that, bent on writing detective fiction, she needed a hero. Lord Peter Wimsey appeared to her "complete with spats and applied [for the job] in an airy don't-care-if-I-don't-get-it" way. In that imaginary interview, he told her a bit about himself—that he was fond of his attractive mother, the Dowager Duchess of Denver, and that he had a gentlemanly manservant whose name was Bunter.

Sayers recounts that she hired Peter Wimsey after the interview and gave him a great deal of money, for it cost her nothing. Actually, in the 1920s, when she began to write her detective tales, she had very little money; therefore, Sayers enjoyed spending her detective's funds to furnish his Piccadilly flat and to buy expensive rare editions. In those days, she would walk to work or ride the bus when she had the fare; in her fiction, she gave Daimlers to Lord Peter.

By 1935, when she wrote that account of her first meeting with Lord Peter to accompany the Harcourt Brace edition of *Gaudy Night*, Dorothy L. Sayers and her whimsical detective were well known in England and the United States. In the 1940s, though, she stopped writing detective novels.

From 1923 to 1936, Sayers wrote and discussed detective fiction. As she developed her craft, she discovered her vision and her voice. She matured in the decades between two world wars, a period that strongly affected her vision. Her popular art gave her a medium to express what she discerned in her society.

When she began to write detective fiction, she wanted to make money and amuse herself. The detective formula suited her. Its tightly controlled plot appealed to her sense of order. The struggle between a concrete good

1

and a concrete evil ending with good's triumph resembled the legends that
she had read as a young girl and continued to study in college. The climatic
scene in detective fiction where the mystery is solved appealed to her love of
drama.

The only child of an Anglican minister, Dorothy L. Sayers was born in
Oxford in 1893. She died in her home in Witham, Essex, in December 1957.
She began her studies under the guidance of her father, the Reverend Henry
Sayers, who was Headmaster of the Cathedral Choir School in Oxford, where
he taught music and Latin. When she was four and a half, the family moved
to the Fen country described in *The Nine Tailors*. There, when she was
seven, her father announced that she was old enough to learn Latin, which
she did. In her early teens, her parents hired a French governess to instruct
her in German and French. By the time she was fifteen she was fluent in
both.

Sayers did not leave home until she was sixteen and entered Godolphin
School, Salisbury, in southern England. There she participated in dramatic
presentations and the debating society. We can find her love for disquisition
in her essays and in such passages as the lengthy dinner conversation in
Gaudy Night. Her character portrayals, as well as her later dramatic produc-
tions for radio and stage, indicate that drama always remained one of her
primary interests. She also sang, wrote poetry, and edited the school magazine. "Youth is important, not for what it is," she said years later, "but for
what it may become. . . ."

In the 1920's, Sayers witnessed the destructive effects on her society of
a world war. Paul Fussell's excellent study, *The Great War and Modern
Memory*, documents the attempt of the British to understand the brutal experience of trench warfare. They had little language to describe the horrors of a
war that was almost within walking distance of the quiet parks and busy
shops of London. They had inherited the language of Shakespearean and
Homeric battles, but a new one was needed. There were no hollow men, no
wasteland metaphors in that legacy. Those metaphors had to be invented to
suit the times, for as Hemingway and others said, the abstractions of honor,
courage, and bravery seemed obscene beside the concrete names of towns
and regiments left in the rubble.

In the clear-headed, unsentimental *Testament of Youth*, written by
Sayers's peer and fellow college student, Vera Brittain, we hear how Brittain
lost her fiancé and her brother, young men of intellectual and artistic promise, and interrupted her security and education at Somerville College to
nurse the wounded.

The first decades of the twentieth century were not civilization's finest, and the time between the wars was one of social upheaval. For detective fiction, however, the period between the wars is known as the Golden Age. The spiritual and moral uncertainties after World War I made the certainties of puzzles with solutions extremely appealing.

Having served in the Great War, Lord Peter is representative of his times; he carries with him the effects of one war and is drawn into a second. He represents not only an energetic solver of puzzles but also the spirit of England. In Sayers's final detective novel, *Busman's Honeymoon*, Harriet Vane, now Lady Wimsey, euphorically thinks to herself, "I have married England." Like Lancelot and other heroes from myth, Wimsey embodies the best qualities of his country.

Sayers realized that her society was in the eye of a spiritual hurricane; this recognition and her ability to express it grew as she pursued her career as a writer of detective fiction.

During the first years of the Great War, Sayers was an undergraduate at Somerville College, Oxford—the model for Shrewsbury College in *Gaudy Night*. She arrived there in 1912 and graduated three years later with First-Class Honors in modern languages and medieval French. Most people who obtained Firsts chose teaching careers. However, like Hilary in *The Nine Tailors*, Sayers wanted to be a writer.

In 1916 and 1918 she published two books of poetry, drawn more from her readings of the classics than from personal, immediate experience. In two poems, however, one can hear her own voice detailing the special experience of Oxford. "Last Morning in Oxford" ends the 1916 collection with a poignant remembrance of the white hemlock by the wall. In "Going-Down Play," she describes the farewell (going-down) songs that she sings gaily, knowing, nonetheless, that tomorrow will bring heartbreak.

Despite Sayers's studiousness and reflective character, Vera Brittain recalls her at Oxford as "a bouncing, exuberant young female who always seemed to be preparing for tea-parties." Energetic, robust—especially as she grew older—humorous, Dorothy Sayers valued vitality of the mind and the body.

After graduation, she went to work with the Oxford publisher of her poetry, Basil Blackwell, where she was known for her cheerfulness, talkativeness, and eagerness to dispute ideas. Her energy harnessed to the tedium of the daily work in which she was engaged caused Blackwell to compare Sayers to a racehorse pulling a coal cart.

At Blackwell's she learned the publishing business as she selected and copy edited manuscripts, skills that came in handy when she edited her

anthologies of detective stories and corrected her own galleys. Besides learning skills, Sayers saw firsthand how the war had affected her society and one
man in particular.

In 1919 she met a young veteran, Eric Whelpton, who had been
wounded and discharged from military service. He had returned to Oxford
University to complete his education, an Oxford that now had 120 male
undergraduates as compared with 3,500 before the war. The four men in his
particular college were there only because of disabilities like his. He recalls
that it took him until 1922 to recover from the effects and that sometimes at
Oxford he passed out several times a day. Undoubtedly Sayers's portraits of
George Fentiman and Peter Wimsey owe much to Eric Whelpton and to
Atherton "Mac" Fleming, whom Sayers married in 1926. Both were subject
to attacks of the nerves, as are Fentiman and Wimsey.

Whelpton and Sayers became close friends. He enjoyed her conversation and admired her knowledge. He claimed that she educated him. She left
Blackwell's to assist him in establishing an office for international exchanges
at the famous École des Roches in Normandy.

During their year there, he recalls, she avidly read cheap novels,
"penny dreadfuls." She invited him to join her and some friends who intended to create a vogue for detective fiction. She promised to make him
famous. Although he refused to participate in her plans, she did fulfill her
promise inadvertently to make him famous, for some have speculated that
Eric Whelpton is the model for Lord Peter Wimsey.

After a brief teaching job, Dorothy Sayers was ready to begin to create
the vogue she promised. She knew the genre; she knew the technical skills of
publishing; she knew her times; she knew Western literature from its beginnings. From 1922 on, she learned to use what she knew.

In 1922, she went to work as a copywriter for S. H. Benson, Ltd., a
large advertising agency in London; she worked there for nine years, while
writing Lord Peter Wimsey short stories and novels in the evenings. Sayers
created much of the copy for one of the most successful advertising cam-
paigns ever to besiege the British—the "Mustard Club." This amusing campaign to promote J. & J. Coleman mustard resembles Lord Peter's Whifflet
ads in *Murder Must Advertise*.

The Mustard Club had a password ("Pass the Mustard, please"), a
badge, an official song, rules, and a cast of characters as entertaining as any
we find in Sayers's fiction. There were the Baron de Beef, Lord Bacon, Lady
Heartly, Phyllis Titmuss, Signor Spaghetti, and Miss Di Gester, all promot-
ing mustard for use in recipes and baths.

Lady Heartly advised young ladies to marry only a Mustard Club member. The police raided the Mustard Club and Baron de Beef and Lord Bacon were indicted for running a secret society. The case was finally dismissed with cheers. The actual secret was that mustard improves digestion. We can detect Sayers's touch in these character sketches and short plots, her levity with a slight satiric bite and characters that appeal to a mass audience.

From S. H. Benson's to her detective fiction to her translations of Dante, she was always a popularizer, in the best sense of that word. Her goal was to reach the people so that they could reach themselves. To stir the soul, to awaken the imagination and the intellect—in other words—to get at what is most exciting about life itself, its creative vitality. This aim underlies her theories about detective fiction, her concern for the importance of well-written popular literature, and her translations. She wanted people to know Dante as a storyteller, to experience the song that died on Roland's lips at the Battle of Roncevaux. *"You cannot,"* she charged, *"stir the soul with abstract nouns."*

As early as 1901, G. K. Chesterton defended the significance of detective fiction. Its characters, he said, resemble the adventurers and villains in Homer and Shakespeare. Like him, Sayers speculated about the significance of the popular genre. She used as one example the series written by a syndicate of writers who appealed to young readers, *The Adventures of Sexton Blake*. "The really interesting point about them," she concluded, "is that they present the nearest modern approach to a national folk-lore, conceived as the centre for a cycle of loosely connected romances in the Arthurian manner."

Detective fiction, then, has its roots in Western mythic tradition. More importantly, Chesterton declared, it is "the earliest and only form of popular literature in which is expressed some sense of the poetry of modern life." Now the city,—its loneliness, its buildings, its lights—becomes as imaginative as any wilderness or sea in epics. Secondly, it redeems our world for us, brings us back to ourselves in wonder at human creativity: "Every brick has as human a hieroglyph as if it were a graven brick of Babylon." Detective fiction reveals "the unfathomably human character in flints and tiles."

Doors are no longer doors, but *doors* with mysteries behind them or significant prints on them. A bed, no longer a bed, speaks of someone's lonely struggle with death by poison.

Because it awakens the reader to his world and stimulates his imagination, detective fiction has "certain definite and real advantages as an agent of the public weal," declared Chesterton. He concluded, "It is good that the average man should fall into the habit of looking imaginatively at ten men in the street even if it is only on the chance that the eleventh might be a notorious thief." In addition to classical structure and drama, then, detective fiction, also appealed to Sayers for its potential to serve a social purpose.

In 1932 twenty-four writers with similar views joined Dorothy Sayers and G. K. Chesterton to found the Detection Club. The Detection Club reacted to the situation that J. B. Priestley saw as a weakness of the age— "nearly all our most sensitive and intelligent writers are completely divorced from popular forms of literature." The Detection Club members vowed to improve popular detective fiction. They also wanted to amuse themselves.

Anthony Berkeley had suggested in 1928 that several writers occasionally dine together to discuss their craft. After several successful gatherings, they decided to form an official club. By 1932, it had a constitution and rules. If it sounds somewhat like the Mustard Club, that may not be coincidental. G. K. Chesterton and Dorothy Sayers are said to have written the election ceremony, which included the new members swearing on Eric the Skull that they would be faithful to the oaths of the Club. They promised to honor the King's English, to reveal clues, but not to depend on "Divine Revelation, Feminine Intuition, Mumbo-Jumbo, Jiggery-Pokery, Coincidence or the Act of God" to solve their cases.

The Club was the "Academy of Detective Arts." It was not a trade union. Its purpose was the improvement of the genre. For that purpose, the members paid nominal dues to maintain their premises at 31 Gerrard Street and an extensive detection library. They also published several works jointly and donated the royalties to the Club.

The first of these, *The Floating Admiral* (1932), lists fourteen contributors. Each introduced complications that the next writer had to consider. Each was bound to work with all that the previous contributor left. In *Ask a Policeman* (1933), six Detection Club members participated. John Rhode supplied a plot for the title; four others provided the solutions; the conclusion was by Milward Kennedy. Their amusement was in speaking through each other's detectives. Anthony Berkeley, for example, wrote Peter Wimsey's solution. These round-robin detective mysteries were games that the members played among themselves as they sharpened their skills.

Sayers participated in these Detection Club publications, which also included *Double Death* (1937) and the anthology *The Anatomy of Murder* (1936), which analyzed actual murder cases. Sayers wrote a long piece on the murder of Mrs. Julia Wallace in which she shows how Mr. Wallace, who was acquitted and later died of cancer, could have been guilty. She also coordinated the Detection Club's participation in radio serials—*Behind the Screen* (1930) and *The Scoop* (1931).

The Club existed to share artistic concerns, skills, and knowledge, as well as amusements. The membership included the best known detective writers of the day. G. K. Chesterton was the first president until his death in 1936. E. C. Bentley replaced him until 1948; Sayers replaced him. She remained president until her death in 1957, when Agatha Christie was elected to the office.

What was begun in 1928 has continued. As the genre has changed, so have the rules and standards. One thing remains the same, however. New members are still elected and initiates still place a hand on Eric the Skull.

During the Golden Age of detective fiction, the Club could speak with clarity and certainty about the difference between "thrillers" and detective novels. Thrillers surprised by shock upon shock. They did not explain; they aimed for emotional effect. The thriller was not the concern of the Detection Club; only detection by logic and fair play concerned them.

In constructing their puzzles, they agreed that the writer must play fair with the reader. This rule was formulated during Sayers's time although, she says, Wilkie Collins had actually practiced the rule long before. Detection Club members were bound by it. It was a tacit contract that made sure that the reader and the detective had an equal chance. The writer must display all of the vital clues, although special, esoteric knowledge was still permissible.

The rule evolved as a result of readers' discontent with passively accepting a detective's brilliant deductions, because they, too, wanted to participate in the detecting. The readers thus placed a burden on the writer, especially as the readers became more educated in the ways of the genre. The writer's problem was to devise ways to fool the reader; the reader's joy was to try to circumvent the writer's success.

In her introduction to *The Floating Admiral*, Sayers paraphrases the rules to which she and her colleagues were bound:

> Put briefly, it amounts to this: that the author pledges himself to play the game with the public and with his fellow-authors. His detectives must detect by their wits, without the help of accident or coincidence; he must not invent impossible death-rays and poisons to produce solutions which no living person could expect; he must write as good English as he can. He must preserve inviolable secrecy concerning his fellow-members' forthcoming plots and titles, and he must give any assistance in his power to members who need advice on technical points.

We can trust Sayers and her contemporaries. Their code of art expressed a code of ethics that from today's perspective is especially appealing.

They were a working community, sharing values, skills, and knowledge. If one had special information, such as timetables, tides, cyphers, she or he would help the others. For example, when she wrote *Have His Carcase*, Sayers called on John Rhode. He helped her with the the Playfair code that Lord Peter and Harriet Vane decipher. He also helped her with the genealogy of the Romanov family and with decisions about the most suitable place for the murder because of the tides. Sayers mentions Rhode in Chapter XXXIII of the novel and acknowledges his help in her prefatory note.

In *The Documents in the Case*, she added the name of Robert Eustace to the cover as co-author. She turned to him for help in specialized knowledge about poisons. His real name was Dr. Eustace Barton. He was a doctor at County Mental Hospital, Gloucester, and under his pseudonym had colaborated with several mystery writers, but he was not a member of the Detection Club.

Sometimes even special help with esoteric knowledge was no guarantee that the writer could outwit all of her readers, however. In a humorous account of the "Trials and Sorrows of a Mystery Writer," Sayers describes how she and Robert Eustace were "let down by a toad stool" in *Documents*. She and Dr. Eustace consulted experts about the behaviors of synthetic and organic poisons. Their plot depended on one's being able to distinguish a difference between the natural and the synthetic poison through a polariscope. Their idea was sound; one could tell a difference. They set to work to murder Mr. Harrison and to convict his murderer. "Well," she recalls, "it wasn't long before we got the inevitable letter from a very polite professor of chemistry, convicting us of a gigantic howler. Our general theory was quite all right, but Muscarin was an exception. Natural Muscarin didn't play fair. It didn't twist the ray of the polarised light any more than the synthetic kind." The ingenious solution turned on a defective point.

She may have let in a few howlers, but Sayers very carefully tried to avoid them. We can trust her sense of fair play and her artistic integrity. Not only did she craft her plots to give the reader a fair chase, she designed them to provoke thought.

Without hesitation, Sayers cautions us in the late 1920s to "make no mistake about it, the detective-story is part of the literature of escape, and not of expression. We read tales of domestic unhappiness because that is the kind of thing which happens to us; but when these things gall too close to the sore, we fly to mystery and adventure because they do not, as a rule, happen to us." By the 1930's, her practice reveals that Sayers had amended her statement. If detective fiction is to have any serious purpose beyond daydreaming, it must bring us back to ourselves. For Sayers, detective fiction became amusement that provokes reflection.

Like the club of writers to which she belonged, Sayers was pledged to amuse her readers, but not to spellbind them. "If there is any serious aim behind the avowedly frivolous organisation of the Detection Club," she said, "it is to keep the detective story up to the highest standard that its nature permits, and to free it from the bad legacy of sensationalism, clap-trap and jargon with which it was unhappily burdened in the past." That statement contains two important phrases: "the highest standard that its nature permits" and "bad legacy of sensationalism."

By concentrating on perfecting a unified design, Sayers countered the bad legacy of thrills with no shape; but she also retained sensations by celebrating the emotions of this world and looking beyond it to the next. Gradually she began to merge the detective novel and the novel of manners. Thus, she could portray ordinary human feelings and social concerns all within an atmosphere of mystery, the essential ingredient of detective fiction.

Sayers wrote in 1930, that the "touchstone . . . is in the word mystery itself. Does the book, or does it not, strike that interior note of essential mysteriousness which is part of the nature of things?" If it does not, it has failed to qualify as a book of the highest standard its nature permits. It was important to Sayers that a popular literary form, especially one that is built on answering questions, evaluate the nature of its questions and their effect on the reader.

The status of the mystery story looked bleak to her in 1930. She feared that it was losing touch with the populace. Although there were many excellent writers, Bentley and Chesterton among them, they were not, like Wilkie Collins a half-century earlier, being read in the kitchens anymore. Detective fiction was being read only "in Downy Street, and in Bloomsbury studios, in bishops' palaces, and in the libraries of eminent scientists." The reason was that the detective novel had become synonymous with the crossword puzzle. It was sacrificing human interest for mechanical problem solving.

In a time of unrest, Sayers saw the potential for the detective novel beyond keeping one's mind frivolously occupied. Because it asks questions about who did it, it could also ask why—questions about moral consciousness and about mortality.

Her works record her attempts to find combinations to bring out the best in detective fiction so that we experience our humanity. She attempted to write so-called escape literature that brings us back to ourselves to reflect upon our powers as well as our limitations. She did not want us to leave her books with a reassurance "that love and hatred, poverty and unemployment, finance and international politics, are problems capable of being dealt with and solved in the same manner as the Death in the Library."

Besides providing her with an income so that she was able to quit her advertising job at Benson's, Sayers's detective writings also provided her with a form in which to experiment with serious questions about social relationships—human puzzles—and the interior note of essential mystery. When she learned all that she could from the detective genre, however, she discarded it.

When Sayers began to write detective fiction in the 1920s, she concentrated on the structure of her craft, more seriously, perhaps, in her novels than in her short stories. But short stories were then the most popular length for detective fiction, and Sayers seems to have written them in order to find out if the short form suited her. We shall see that it was the longer form of the novel that showed her the potential that she could reach and the questions that she could ask within the conventions of the detective genre.

1

BETWEEN THE SEA
AND A PRECIPICE:
SAYERS'S DETECTIVE
SHORT STORIES
Lord Peter Views the Body
Hangman's Holiday
In the Teeth of the Evidence

The writer of detective fiction, according to Sayers, can turn neither the plot nor the characters loose. Both she and E. C. Bentley contrasted the detective writer's approach with that of a nonformulaic writer, John Galsworthy. He claimed that he sat in a chair, pipe in his mouth, pen in his hand, and waited for his characters to find their way. For the characters in detective fiction, Sayers pointed out, the future is fixed. They must obey the laws of the plot as well as their own. They cannot, she asserted quoting Galsworthy, "kick free of swaddling clothes and their creators." The detective writer must be very careful, then, in choosing the appropriate character-plot combination. The effort, Bentley said, was so crushing that his title *Trent's Last Case* was conceived with the intention of never writing another detective novel, an intention, we might add, he did not hold to.

Sayers explained the detective writer's situation. First, one may have an idea for an opening scene, such as the discovery of a body in a bathtub, or an idea for an ingenious way to murder the victim. Secondly, the writer must begin to think about how to shape the idea, how to introduce it, how to introduce the investigator, how to present the clues and to explain their significance, how to reveal the criminal so that all the clues will seem, upon reflection, to be self-evident. At the end of the work, the reader should feel as though he ought to have known the direction the clues were taking him. Ideas to surprise her increasingly detective-wise audience were becoming fewer, however. "We are older and warier now," Sayers declared in 1934, "and nothing surprises us very much."

In order to keep the reader interested, then, Sayers recognized that the detective-fiction writer must wisely use her space. She explained that one of

11

the most difficult problems that faces the writer is how best to use her central idea—the surprising discovery of a body or an ingenious murder—so that it is not wasted.

In order not to waste the precious idea, which could not be repeated, the writer must "decide whether the thing will bear the superstructure which he will have to heap upon it to bring it up to novel length; or whether, on the other hand, if he tries to tell the whole story in six thousand words, the necessary complications will not reduce his story to a huddled and incomprehensible summary." If the puzzle is too complicated, there may be little or no story; however, if the story introduces too much material that is extraneous to the puzzle, then an interesting idea will be wasted.

But despite such restrictions, Sayers published, between 1925 and 1939, forty-three short stories. (Her forty-fourth, "Talboys," was written in 1942, found in 1961, and published in 1972.) Half of her short stories feature Lord Peter Wimsey; ten introduce a second detective, Montague Egg. Of the remaining twelve miscellaneous pieces, few can properly be called detective stories. Some playfully use the characteristics of the detective formula ("The Inspiration of Mr. Budd," "The Milk Bottles," "An Arrow O'er the House," and "The Man That Knew How") or of the horror story ("Scrawns"). Others are tales of ethics ("Dilemma" and "Blood Sacrifice") or unsolvable mysteries ("The Cyprian Cat" and "The Leopard Lady"). Another emphasizes the psychology of the guilty person in the manner of Edgar Allan Poe's "The Tell-Tale Heart" ("Nebuchadnezzar").

Sayers's first collection of short stories, *Lord Peter Views the Body* (1928), features only Lord Peter. In her second collection in 1933, when Montague Egg appeared, Wimsey had almost disappeared from the short form. Only eight out of twenty-nine short stories from 1932 to 1939 featured Lord Peter.

An author had to be careful indeed when choosing to write a detective short story. The writer must introduce its complication quickly, bring in the detective usually simultaneously with the complication, and resolve it in a way that the reader will not feel cheated. These technical considerations for short-story writers in Sayers's day were made more difficult by editorial restrictions. First, she said, the magazine editor insists on "the fair, spotless maiden, and her bronzed and chivalrous lover. To add to the difficulty, he demands that the murder, if there has to be a murder, should have nothing morbid or unpleasant about it." And secondly, not only were there restrictions on content, but editors also imposed them on length.

At one time, publishers would accept only 70,000 to 80,000 words for a novel; by 1931–34, they had begun to publish novels up to 120,000 words in length. As the novel's length increased, the short story's decreased. In the early thirties, an editor who used to accept 10,000 words for a short story would take no more than 6,000. To corroborate Sayers's figures, we can look at *Writing for the Press* (1935) by Leonard Russell, which lists the lengths of all types of short stories in British newspapers; the longest was 3,000 words.

The detective novel, on the other hand, had fewer restrictions. It could offer its readers interesting characters as well as a merry chase, both of which needed space to develop. Because of the restrictions on length and content as well as the increasingly sophisticated audience, the detective short story was, in Sayers's words, "in the position of a city built between the sea and a precipice." On one side, editorial policies about length were nibbling away at the short story; on the other, preferences for traditionally sentimental plots and characters were preventing its necessary evolution.

About plot, Sayers cautioned that the detective short story must put "all its eggs in one basket; it can turn one trick and one trick only; its detective-interest cannot involve a long investigation—it must be summed up in a single surprise." In the steadily decreasing space of an already short story, the characters must be sketchy at best. Also, the puzzle cannot be complicated. There is no room, as Lord Peter says, for "long and twaddly and tedious" conversation in order to tease the puzzle along or to reveal personalities.

To Sayers, who refused to displace character in favor of puzzle, the situation presented a special problem that Chesterton wittily identified. In a short murder story "even the living characters may be left at the end looking rather like conventional corpses." One solution Sayers advised was "the detective with well-defined mannerisms."

In an unpublished essay, Sayers talks about the difficulty of getting the detective going. If one chooses a complete free-lancer, she may have to put up with coincidence; if one chooses a detective with a full-time job, she must find a way for him to abandon it. For her short stories Sayers chose two detectives who plausibly complete the necessary detecting action of the conventional form. For her free-lance detective, Lord Peter, Sayers found coincidences that fit his position. He sometimes hears a story on a train or in a restaurant, a story about which he wants to learn more. His freedom and wealth allow him to indulge his curiosity. As a full-time travelling salesman, Sayers's other detective, Montague Egg, has a reason to travel and thus to encounter problems.

Lord Peter can devote months to a case, even journeying to a remote area in the Pyrenees. His travels are determined only by his whimsey; Monty's, by his job as commercial traveller for Plummet & Rose, Wines and

Spirits, Piccadilly. He can spare time from his busy schedule of selling wine only to listen to evidence and to arrive at a conclusion. Even the truncated structures of the shortest Egg stories are consistent with his character. He has no time to see the criminal caught or his conclusions substantiated. His schedule suits the requisite one trick of the detective short story. In these tales of 4,000 to 4,500 words, Montague Egg works quickly.

Not only are the plots that Sayers structures appropriate for the circumstances of the main characters, the detectives Lord Peter and Montague Egg fulfill their creator's theory that in the short story the detective with well-defined mannerisms does best.

By 1928, the year of Sayers's first short story collection, her aristocratic detective had already appeared in four novels. Readers were therefore familiar with his habits of buying rare editions and of drinking café au lait for breakfast. They knew his speech, which mingles Shakespeare and nursery rhymes, and his dress, which no longer includes spats but instead, a monocle and a walking stick.

While Lord Peter disappears from more and more of the short stories, Montague Egg first enters in the collection *Hangman's Holiday* (1933) and remains in *In the Teeth of Evidence* (1939). His mannerisms and habits become as well known as his aristocratic counterpart's.

Lord Peter inserts his monocle; Mr. Egg waves his smart trilby. Wimsey resonates "Lord Peter Bredon Death Wimsey";* Egg humbly murmurs just plain "Monty." Peter drives a series of Daimlers; Monty, a practical Morris. Lord Peter smokes cigars, cigarettes, pipes. Montague Egg shakes his head reproachfully at cigar smoking. (He does smoke a cigarette.) Wimsey often says, "Oh, damn!" and "Hell!" Egg's strongest expletive is "Dash it."

In an unpublished manuscript in the Marion Wade Collection at Wheaton College, Sayers explains that the exaggerated mannerisms that sometimes tire the readers are the tricks by which the character survives at first. In the detective work, the character is so busy following clues that he has little room to contemplate his inner life. Until he is sufficiently familiar, the author must rely on distinctive behavior to keep the detective alive in the readers' minds. After he is well known, however, these physical traits become part of his enduring image.

---

*Wimsey tells a character in *Murder Must Advertise* (1933) that his name is "spelt Death. Pronounce it any way you like. Most of the people who are plagued with it make it rhyme with teeth, but personally I think it sounds more picturesque when rhymed with breath."

For a detective to be truly great, Sayers writes in "Other People's Great Detectives," he must have presence. In her essay, she uses Sergeant Cuff of Wilkie Collins's *The Moonstone* as her example. We recall his sharp, melancholy face that almost smiles at times. "Then comes the unexpected revelation of a private humanity in the pursuit of a favorite hobby." We never doubt his humanity, she affirms, because we believe Cuff intensely loves to raise roses.

Sayers's short stories do not reveal Montague Egg's inner world. We come to know what Egg's values are, however—honor and sales psychology. He represents the best of the commercial world, which often greedily exploits employer and consumer. But only briefly when his face puckers do we catch a glimpse of what one could call a "private humanity." Building on the character that she had begun in the short, short stories, Sayers could have possibly given Montague Egg greatness as well as personality.

Comparing the Wimsey and Egg stories, the fuller plots of Wimsey's tend to be more satisfying, although Monty Egg often emerges as the more lovable character of the two. He is a secular Father Brown; his Bible, the *Salesman's Handbook*; his commandments, aphorisms about sales strategy. Because of her training in commerce and advertising, Sayers doubtlessly enjoyed creating the maxims that Egg quotes. His favorite motto, a rephrasing of Horace's poetics that poetry should delight and instruct, appears in "One Too Many": "Speak the truth with cheerful ease if you would both convince and please."

In the short stories, the world of Montague Egg is closer to Everyman's than is Wimsey's. Egg frequents commercial rooms of various roadside pubs instead of Wimsey's ubiquitous clubs. His is a world that hints at a dark "poetry of modern life," to use Chesterton's phrase, a world of selling, rootlessness, geniality for a pound or dollar. It foreshadows the world that we have learned from Arthur Miller's *Death of a Salesman*. No Willy Loman, however, Mr. Egg, with his sample case of wine catalogues, merrily wanders into situations of fraud and murder, observes, evaluates, and departs cheerfully.

Although he moves about in the diminishing territory of the short, short story, Montague Egg retains a consistent character. His characteristics and activities and the stories' designs originate in his vocation as a commercial traveller. His rosy face puckers with distress when he discovers that one of his customers has been poisoned in "Bitter Almonds" and "The Poisoned Dow '08." In the first story he recalls something that he had read about the liqueur, a recollection that solves the case. In the second, he notices the significant clue, a bottle that is not from Plummett & Rose.

To be successful as a salesman, Monty Egg has learned to be observant. In "Sleuths on the Scent," his observations detect a wanted murderer. Similarly, his keen scrutiny of his fellow passengers in "One Too Many" helps to solve the mystery of a wealthy—and criminal—financier's disappearance. When Chief Inspector Peacock compliments him, Monty replies complacently that to be observant is his job.

In addition to the action, the structure of the Egg stories is consistent with the amateur detective's character. Appropriate for a travelling salesman who cannot linger in one place too long, his stories are beginnings and middles. They stop before Egg and the reader see his ratiocination substantiated and the criminal brought to justice.

"Murder at Pentecost," which anticipates *Gaudy Night*, is set in Oxford. The story begins with Monty's overhearing the upperclassman Radcott reprimand his junior classmate for using the unsophisticated word "'undergrads' like a ruddy commercial traveller." With an apologetic cough, Mr. Egg enters the action. His motto "ready to learn means ready to earn" motivates him to ask the Oxford man for the acceptable word, so that he will not be spotted immediately as an outsider.

The murder in the story depends on an outsider's ability to use college protocol to disguise his actual purpose, which is to kill the Master of Pentecost College. Another ousider, Monty Egg, solves the case—at least we assume that he does. This story, balanced thematically on the motif of the outsider, is structurally cut short. It ends after Egg speculates about who could have killed the Master of Pentecost. Egg recalls the tale of the man who cried, "Wolf!" He concludes that the murderer is the Most Unlikely Person, who confesses to every murder committed in town. We assume that he is correct.

In "Dirt Cheap," he concludes that the Most Likely Person did it. Egg awakens from his sleep on a lumpy bed in a dusty hotel to the ugly sounds of someone's strangling. When he knocks on the door of his fellow travelling salesman, Mr. Pringle, he hears a reply assuring him that the occupant is all right. The next morning the maid discovers that Mr. Pringle is dead and his sample case of jewels has been stolen. The motif of dirt—the condition of the hotel and the code of the murderer—forms the design of the story. The killer, who sleeks his hair down and looks like the stereotypical villain, sells dirty pictures under the guise of enlarging family photos "dirt cheap." Appropriately, Monty finds the significant clue to the villain's crime in the dust of Mr. Pringle's night table.

The theme of dirty commerce occurs in two other stories. By contrast with the virtuous Egg, the criminals in "The Professor's Manuscript" and "One Too Many" abscond with funds and attempt to hide by disguising themselves. In "The Professor's Manuscript," Mr. Egg observes that the professor arranges his books according to size rather than subject; also, he puts his books too tightly on the shelf. From his experience with scholarly customers, Egg concludes that Professor Pindar is a fraud. In "One Too Many," Monty notices that a bearded foreigner seems to smoke his cigars unnaturally fast. He must therefore be more than one person. Monty then concludes that Simon Grant, the missing financier, had assumed another identity that had been arranged several years earlier so that he could disappear with impunity.

The short stories that feature Montague Egg present their puzzles and solutions quickly and reasonably. The actions begin plausibly with a situation in the world of commerce. Egg's method of deducing solutions is consistent with his vocation as a salesman who observes people closely in order to make a sale. By using his senses intelligently, he uncovers the significant relationships among the appearances in his world. Only once does he depend solely on his imagination to solve a crime.

In "Maher-Shalal-Hashbaz," courteous Mr. Egg helps a shabbily dressed teenager rescue her cat. She wants to answer an advertisement that promises ten shillings in exchange for the right cat. Mr. Egg helps young Jean Maitland sell her pet to Mr. Doe; however, he never completely relaxes about the strange ad and the circumstances of selling the cat.

A week later when he visits the Maitlands, the cat Maher-Shalal-Hashbaz—better known as Mash—has come home. When Jean tries to return Mr. Doe's check, the letter comes back marked "not known." Monty Egg considerately delivers the check to the house where Mr. Doe had received the cat. The caretaker shows Monty more than fifty dead cats buried in a shallow grave.

From the caretaker, Egg learns that Mr. Doe, whose real name is Mr. Proctor, left the house after his wealthy uncle, with a look of horror upon his face, died of heart failure. In his imagination, Egg re-creates the scene of what happened—the cats, the locked room, the old, sick man, the listener outside the door. The pieces add up to a story to tell the police, and Egg's decision to tell them ends the story.

For the reader, Egg's imaginative creation is proof enough, just as Sayers's imaginative creations in the other stories convince us that Egg's conclusions are correct. Although we never know empirically whether or not

Egg is right, we have faith that he is; we have faith in the artist's design. "If the imagination is consistent," Sayers says much later, "the work will produce effects *as if* it were actually true." The consistency of her imagination in the Montague Egg stories effectively substitutes single tricks for long investigations and demonstrates the efficacy of the artist's imagination. After Egg announces his conclusion and the story ends, we can supply the denouement. We may not be pleased that we must, but we never doubt that we can.

In addition to reasonable, although foreshortened plots, Sayers creates a memorable character that lives in harmony with the narrow landscape of the short story. Still, one does like to ponder what could have happened had Mr. Egg's creator given him a vacation. Or what would have happened if chubby-faced Monty Egg had crossed over from his employ at Messrs. Plummett & Rose of Piccadilly, *Salesman's Handbook* under his arm, to 110A Piccadilly to make a sales call on a monocled, lean-faced gentleman eagerly bending his long nose over a rare manuscript of Justinian.

Their meeting is plausible, but by 1933 when Egg appeared in the short stories, Wimsey had almost disappeared from the short form. Although Lord Peter was still to appear in a few short stories, over the next five years Sayers primarily developed his character within the more elaborate framework of the novel.

The short stories, however, gave her a chance to experiment with Lord Peter's nature. While Montague Egg represents ethical values in the world of business, Peter Wimsey supplies an almost religious force in the secular world. The stories emphasize his godlike presence and abilities. The most obvious examples are "The Abominable History of the Man with Copper Fingers" and "The Incredible Elopement of Lord Peter Wimsey." In the former, Wimsey saves Varden—a young, athletic, innocent film star—from a gruesome death. In the second story, he saves a beautiful woman. In both he magically appears.

"The Abominable History of the Man with Copper Fingers" achieves its effect by having two narrators. First, to the members of the Egoists's Club, Varden presents his account of a strange event. Then Wimsey explains and completes the tale. The structure strengthens the hint of mysteriousness by presenting events first from Varden's limited point of view.

He tells how he met the sculptor Loder, and his almost perfectly shaped mistress, Maria Moreno, in New York before the first world war. Maria and Varden became friends. After the war, Varden again visited Loder and began to sit for him. Loder tells Varden Maria has left him. As the sculptor works, he tells Varden shockingly vulgar things. On his last evening in New York, Varden waits alone for Loder in the smoking room. Suddenly, Varden becomes aware of someone's presence in the room, a young man with "a curious, hesitating, husky voice and a strong English accent." The voice warns him to flee from the house or, like Maria Moreno, he would *never* leave it.

After Varden finishes his account, the voice comes out of the shadows behind Varden's chair. It huskily explains that the lifesized nude figure of a woman that formed the perverse couch of silver in the room where Varden awaited Loder was Maria. The jealously insane artist had also planned a figure of Varden to be entitled *The Sleeping Athlete*. The voice is Lord Peter's. He explains how he happened to deduce Loder's plan and what happened after Varden ran from the house.

Both "The Abominable History" and "The Incredible Elopement of Lord Peter Wimsey" dramatize the destructive effects of jealousy, especially of a person in power. In the beginning of the second story, the ethnologist Professor Langley arrives in the Pyrenees on the trail of Basque folklore for his book. Coincidentally, a former acquaintance, the doctor Standish Wetherall, lives in this isolated area with his wife. The inhabitants tell Langley that the Evil One has bewitched Mrs. Wetherall, who changed from a beautiful woman to a hideous, nonhuman, drooling monster. When the two men meet, Standish taunts Langley, accusing him of desiring his wife, and gloats that in her present state no would want her.

Fortunately for Alice Wetherall, Langley meets Lord Peter on a train going to Paris. Being interested in strange things, Wimsey listens to the scholar's tale. The scene then shifts to the middle of November in the Basque village where a wizard has just arrived. His white magic, a combination of Greek and Latin poetry and Schubert's music, saves Alice Wetherall from her husband. Wimsey arranges her escape on the ship *Abracadabra* and leaves the Basque peasants a new legend to tell to studious ethnologists.

In "The Abominable History" and "The Incredible Elopement," Wimsey fights crimes against beauty. In the former, he is too late to save the nearly perfectly shaped Maria Moreno, but he saves the handsome athlete. In the latter, he arrests the degenerative humiliation of Mrs. Wetherall, "that delicate piece of golden womanhood" by bringing her the necessary medicine for her thyroid condition, medicine that her husband denied her. Both the scientist of one story and the artist of the other violate the creative powers of their knowledge. In contrast, welding the magic of poetry, music, and science, Wimsey vanquishes those who misuse knowledge and beauty.

Sometimes this conqueror of destruction and evil appears as if by magic, as in the above stories or in "Striding Folly," where he arrives after a thunderstorm. Sometimes he slips up to the scene, silently, as in "The

Fantastic Horror of the Cat in the Bag." In "The Adventurous Exploit of the
Cave of Ali Baba," he returns from the dead. Mrs. Ruyslaender of "The
Unprincipled Affair of the Practical Joker" believes that divine intervention
leads her to Wimsey. Then, as she seeks his suite in the hotel, "a large
golden arrow at the corner directed her to Suite 24."

Although she associates Lord Peter with magic and divinity, Sayers
playfully undermines his omniscience to keep him human. Certainly, he
often looks unheroic. In "The Undignified Melodrama of the Bone of Conten-
tion," he hunches his shoulders like "a dilapidated heron." He even moans
about his looks in "The Unprincipled Affair of the Practical Joker." After all
the build-up to see her rescuer, Mrs. Ruyslaender hears him say, "It's very
tryin', you can't think, always to look as if one's name was Algy." In "The
Abominable History," Varden describes his rescuer as "exceptionally ordinary looking," with "sleek, pale hair, and one of those rather stupid faces."
To Langley in "The Incredible Elopement," Lord Peter seems friendly, but
he does "not look particularly intelligent." Even nature sometimes pesters
him, as in "The Undignified Melodrama" when he breaks off a branch of ivy:
"The plant shuddered revengefully, tipping a small shower of water down
Wimsey's neck." Algy or Lord, wet neck or dry, his presence suggests rescue.

By solving difficult puzzles, he not only aids people financially, he also
adds a dimension to their spirits. To the overly serious, he brings joy; to the
overly scientific, he brings the mysterious. He also enables the dead to live
again through their wills.

In "The Fascinating Problem of Uncle Meleager's Will," with the help
of his sister Mary, Lord Peter deciphers Meleager Finch's crossword puzzle
to find his will. Meleager's legacy includes money to his niece, Hannah,
whose mother needs an operation and a health cure abroad. Equally as important as providing money for Hannah, Uncle Meleager's will brings the
frivolity of puzzle solving into this serious young woman's life. And by deci-
phering the will and finding the buried treasure of Cut-Throat the pirate
("The Learned Adventure of the Dragon's Head"), Lord Peter introduces
Cut-Throat's scientific heir, Dr. Conyers, to the value of astrology. After they
find the buried treasure, the scientist, who can now build his cancer research
hospital, admits that before this adventure he had considered astrology a
waste of time.

Like old Cut-Throat Conyers and nasty Uncle Meleager, Joseph Alexan-
der Ferguson in "The Piscatorial Farce of the Stolen Stomach" demonstrates
a sense of humor that continues after his death. His heir, also a scientist,

inherits the riches of his uncle's vitality—his stomach. After a life of good health, Uncle Joseph had a stroke, recognized that the end was near and, at the age of ninety-five, committed suicide by jumping out of a sixty-storey window. Lord Peter wonders why the old man would leave his great nephew his stomach. Reading the will carefully to determine the mood of its author, Lord Peter discovers the answer and the fortune in diamonds that Uncle Joseph swallowed.

Peter Wimsey's curiosity, his ability to see beyond the literal and to identify with all three testators give him the power to synthesize information. He not only recognizes the intellectual and imaginative vitality of the dead men, he enables them to share it. Like Poe's Dupin, Wimsey uses his intellect creatively.

In one of Sayers's best short stories, "The Unsolved Puzzle of the Man With No Face," we find that Lord Peter's ability as a storyteller is as effective as his creative detecting. A man is found dead at the beach. One of the suspects is a professional partner at a public dance hall. (The story looks forward to *Have His Carcase*.) Another suspect is Mr. Crowder, a commercial artist who works for an advertising agency, Crichton's. The victim, Mr. Coreggio Plant, took credit for others' work and, on the whole, was thoroughly despicable.

Using his power as studio manager, Plant insisted that Mr. Crowder paint his portrait. An artist, Crowder had taken the commercial job to make money so that he could get married. By asking Crowder to paint his portrait, Plant had "forgotten that, however much an artist will put up with in the ordinary way, he is bound to be sincere with his art. That's the one thing a genuine artist won't muck with," says Lord Peter, who enunciates one of Sayers's consistent themes about integrity. Crowder rendered Plant as sinister and unvirtuous as he was. The enmity between the two gives Crowder a motive for murder; a young woman's rejection of the professional dancer for Plant introduces a second suspect.

The story begins on a train with a group of people discussing the murder. As in many stories, Lord Peter remains an unnamed presence for the first part of the telling. Called only "the first-class passenger," he refutes the other passengers' speculations about the murderer being an ex-soldier gone mad or a member of a secret organization. From the facts in the newspaper, the first-class passenger deduces that the murder took place before high tide; that the murderer mysteriously came out of the sea; that the murder method was strangulation—"the characteristic British way"; and that the final act of violence was a furious slashing of Plant's face with whatever the murderer could find on the beach. The anonymous passenger surmises also how the murderer got away and what the police ought to look for—a garage with a car that someone will call for. At the end of the train ride, this passenger produces his card: LORD PETER WIMSEY/110A PICCADILLY. Like an incantation, the words intimate that the speculations will be proven correct.

Indeed, the middle of the story validates the theory of the car in the garage and the details of the seascape. Up to this point, Wimsey seems to be infallible. Thus, at the end of the story when Lord Peter snuggles into his armchair to answer Who? How? Why? we are prepared to accept his answers.

He begins his explanation to Inspector Winterbottom by introducing his account as a fairy story. True to convention, he begins, "Once upon a time . . . there was a painter. He was a good painter, but the bad fairy of Financial Success had not been asked to his christening," and so forth. We listen and believe in the truth of this story, which Lord Peter dramatizes by getting into the role of the painter. He describes the day of the murder, the two men, the water's chuckling sound as it swirled around their feet, the painter's reactions to the dead man's face, his creation of a new one with the edges of a broken bottle.

Had Sayers ended the story right here, we would feel discontent because of an unfinished structure (as we do sometimes in not knowing for *sure* in the Monty Egg stories) but we would trust Wimsey's account. We are allowed full satisfaction, however—beginning, middle, and a very definite ending. The Inspector, who has been laughing during Lord Peter's telling, reveals that although it was a fine story the painter did not kill Mr. Plant.

After Inspector Winterbottom departs, Wimsey thoughtfully gazes at the portrait Crowder had painted. The story ends with Peter's reflecting aloud that he could prove the painter's guilt if he wanted to, but Plant "had a villainous face, and there are few good painters in the world." And, after all, what is truth? he asks. The "unsolved puzzle" of the title refers, then, not to the puzzle plot, but to that final question. It is a question that *Clouds of Witness* and *The Documents in The Case* implicitly ask and that humanity always asks. Certainly, it is a pertinent question for detective fiction.

In three of her miscellaneous short stories, Dorothy Sayers seems to relish showing the consequences of mistaken trust in one's conclusions about what is true. She achieves humorous effects in "An Arrow O'er the House," "The Milk-Bottles," and "The Man That Knew How" by constructing characters who trust their imaginations too much. They lack the creative balance of imagination and reason of a Peter Wimsey.

In "The Man That Knew How," we first meet the main character, Mr. E. Pender, on the train reading a penny dreadful. His travelling companion's staring makes him nervous. He cannot concentrate on his novel, *Murder in the Manse*. He offers the traveller, Mr. Smith, another of his books, *The Paper Clip Clue*, and apologetically admits that these books lack characterization and human interest. Not interested in the literary value of detective novels, however, Mr. Smith prefers to discuss the incompetence of fictional murderers whom he finds boring. His cold documentary objectivity excites Mr. Pender who has apparently read too many mysteries while riding on trains.

The next day, Pender reads an article about a bathtub murder in Rugby, where his acquaintance had departed from the train. From that moment, Pender becomes overly concerned about baths. He begins to take cooler ones. He attends inquests of bathtub deaths and on one occasion, he again meets Mr. Smith. They have a drink together. Mr. Smith seems suspiciously interested in Pender, who then begins to think that he is in danger.

The story reaches its climax on a cold, foggy night. Pender hears footsteps behind him, but he is prepared. He strikes and his pursuer falls. Mr. Smith, Pender learns too late, was not who he appeared to be, thus Sayers introduces a variation on the classic formula, the Most Unlikely Person.

Like Mr. Pender, the young reporter of "The Milk-Bottles" (and of *Murder Must Advertise*), Hector Puncheon, leaves reason behind as he allows his imagination to lead him on a trail of false clues. Unopened milk bottles begin to collect outside the apartment of Mr. and Mrs. Hugh Wilbraham. A neighbor has overheard Mr. Wilbraham speaking sharply to his wife. Then Mr. Wilbraham is seen leaving the apartment with a suitcase in his hand. No one has seen his wife.

Ever watchful for a story, Hector writes a short article about the mysterious milk bottles and the missing couple. Another newspaper embellishes the story. Hector investigates further. The clues, including a nauseating stench, point to a sinister conclusion. We find, however, that Hector, like Mr. Pender, has let his imagination lead him astray. The story ends with a delightfully commonsensical explanation.

In "An Arrow O'er the House," where she also presents overly imaginative characters, Sayers has some fun with the publishing and the advertising professions. Mr. Humphrey Podd has just completed a novel, *The Time Will Come*. He asks his secretary rhetorically, now that the book has been completed, what are they to do with it? Send it to the publisher and let it remain in its humble brown paper? He decides, no; his time has come. He will call attention to his work by some advertising gimmick. He therefore mails sinister excerpts from his book to the publisher, Mr. Milton Ramp, to whom he plans to announce the fiction at a propitious moment.

One day, Mr. Podd and a fellow writer are lunching when Mr. Ramp enters the restaurant. He looks awful, the result of having received some disconcerting letters. Ah, thinks Mr. Podd, Mr. Ramp will be so relieved when he finds out that the excerpts are not threats but are from a novel. Mr. Podd concludes that Mr. Ramp will certainly ask him to write another novel and begins to prepare a sequel.

Like Mr. Pender and Hector Puncheon, however, Mr. Podd relies on his imaginative conclusions instead of validating them with facts. To complicate the story, Mr. Podd's secretary also lets her imagination dictate to her, resulting in a doubly surprising and humorous ending to the story.

In their plots about detection, these stories are only tangentially related to Sayers's detective fiction. In her stories that follow the conventional pattern, however, we can see how Sayers accepted the challenge of telling a detective short story, a form that in her day had fallen on hard times.

She concentrated on unified design and consistency of character in even her shortest of stories, Montague Egg's. We believe in Monty Egg, his code of ethical behavior and in his way of solving puzzles. "Don't trust to luck, but be exact and verify the smallest fact," Mr. Egg advises in "Murder in the Morning." In creating him, Sayers drew a believable portrait by means of consistency. Egg lives in a world of commercial facts—when a particular wine was bottled, how many bottles were sold, what time the trains leave London. Educated to notice such things, Egg uses his training to solve puzzles. His background and his virtuous nature convince the reader to have faith in Egg's ratiocination even when we never see the consequences of his conclusions.

We also believe in the truth of Lord Peter Wimsey. His imaginative ingenuity is consistent with his appearing mysteriously in New York to rescue a young man or in the Pyrenees to rescue a beautiful woman and leaving on the *Abracadabra*. Lord Peter of the short stories often combines the "other world" of magic and divinity with this world. He brings us closer than Monty Egg to the essential mysteriousness of life: life after death (in the stories about wills and testaments), the magic of science, and the horrors of love. As we shall discover, the Peter Wimsey of the novels retains some of this combination of this world and another.

In order to range this world, however, Dorothy Sayers's imagination needed a broader landscape than the detective short story allowed.

2

THE DESIGN OF THE GLITTERING MECHANISM: SAYERS'S DETECTIVE NOVELS OF THE 1920s

Whose Body?, Clouds of Witness
Unnatural Death
The Unpleasantness at the Bellona Club

As she wrote her first detective novels in the 1920s, Sayers surveyed her territory. She noted Edgar Allan Poe's importance to the art of detection and Sir Arthur Conan Doyle's after him.

Poe created the patterns for the surprise ending. In "Thou Art the Man," he introduced the Most Unlikely Person, in "The Murders in the Rue Morgue," the Unexpected Means.* His characters of C. Auguste Dupin and the anonymous narrator provided the models for later detectives and their admiring helpers. One of the most famous of the duos was, of course, Sherlock Holmes and Dr. Watson.

Sayers's own detective, Peter Wimsey, with his hawklike profile, bears some physical similarity to Holmes, whom he also intellectually resembles. His creative intelligence also was inherited from Dupin.

Without dismissing the importance of Doyle's and Poe's influences on detective fiction, Sayers spoke for a change. She differed from the creators of Dupin and Holmes in their emphasis on the puzzle. On the other hand, Sayers was aligned with Poe in his aesthetics. Poe advocated Aristotle's unities of time, place, and action in his famous pronouncement about the short story. In his review of Hawthorne's short stories in the 1840s, he mandated, "In the whole composition there should be no word written, of which

---

*For a discussion of Poe's influence, see, in addition to Sayers's introduction to *Great Short Stories of Detection, Mystery and Horror* (1928), John G. Cawelti's *Adventure, Mystery, and Romance* (Chicago: University of Chicago Press, 1976), Chapter 4.

the tendency, direct or indirect is not to the one pre-established design."
Poe's insistence on unity brought Aristotle's aesthetics of the drama to prose
fiction. Like Poe, Sayers also adhered to the concept of aesthetic unity. "To
get the central idea" is one thing for the writer, she insisted, but "to surround
it with a suitable framework of interlocking parts is quite another."

By "design" Poe meant more than the sequence of the action. He literally meant that every word written should contribute to the total emotional
and intellectual effect of a short story (and, by extension, a novel). In this, he
and Sayers agreed.

Doyle was not as careful in his creation. Sayers pointed out, "As regards the past of his characters, Conan Doyle's imagination was not, in fact,
very consistent; there are lapses and contradictions, as well as lacunae."
Such lapses remind us that Sherlock Holmes is not a "real" person, a reality
that apparently did not interest Doyle. Holmes is a made-up character who
exists to solve puzzles and to solve them in the short story. Sayers had addi-
tional aims.

She cautioned the imitators of Poe and Doyle to remember that the
supersleuths, Dupin and Holmes, were products of the short form, which
because of its length gave precedence to puzzle-solving. By relying on the
models of Poe and Doyle, detective novelists were therefore merely produc-
ing expanded short stories "with a twist in the tail." They were not considering the nature of a novel.

Following the example of Wilkie Collins in *The Moonstone* instead of
Poe or Doyle, Sayers meant for her detective fiction to develop as novels, not
as expanded short stories. Novelists, she declared, consider plot as part of a
larger social pattern that includes characters and setting. They "never
present the story as an isolated episode existing solely in virtue of its relation
to the mechanics of detection. They are interested in the social background,
in manners and morals, in the depiction and interplay of character."

Without sacrificing the unity of the mechanical design of the puzzle
plot, Sayers wanted to broaden the context of the puzzle to include the social
background and the relationship among characters. Together puzzle and its
social context could be shaped to contribute to the overall emotional and
intellectual effect of the novel.

Sayers's aesthetics, which developed as she practiced her art, were
based on the belief that art mirrors society, but first and more importantly, on
the belief that art shapes experience, the writer's and the reader's.

If someone asks what one of Sayers's novels is about, we more than
likely answer that it is about a woman who was killed so that her niece could

inherit a fortune, or it is about a man who was murdered by his wife's lover. Then we summarize the plot. As fundamental as it is, plot, as we summarize it, is not what affects us as we read, nor is the moral—if there is one.

After she had ceased writing novels, Sayers explained what she believed was the experience of art in "Towards a Christian Aesthetic" (in *Unpopular Opinions*). She said that in *Agamemnon*, Aeschylus is telling us something, but it is something more than the story of a sensational murder of a husband by his adulterous wife. The synopsis of the story recounts the event, but not the reader's or the writer's experience of that event. What affects us is the creative happening. Aeschylus's whole work communicates a design in the making. In following it, the audience relives the author's creation. Ideally, then, to answer the question of what the work is about, the artist would hand us the play or the novel and say, "Read it. It is about itself being made."

Since that will not do, we can turn to Sayers's contemporary, E. M. Forster. In *Aspects of the Novel* (1927), he used the now well-known examples of "The king died and then the queen died" to illustrate the term *story* and "The king died, and then the queen died of grief" to illustrate *plot*. He recognized that he had not said enough, however, for he included with plot not only causal relationships, but also relationships of comparison and contrast. Specifically, Forster explained the reader's experience as an activity involving intelligence and memory. The story emphasizes what happens next; plot, how and why it happens. Story appeals to the reader's curiosity; plot, to the reader's reflective creativity that engages the reader's intelligence and memory.

Detection pulls us through the novel (Aha! The poison was in the chicken. No, it must have been on the napkin.) As we advance along the trail of our suspicion, we also begin to notice how repeated motifs and juxtapositions of passages form patterns of meaning beyond how the poison was administered.

In Sayers's novels, meaning taking shape tells us something more than who did it. Her novels of the 1930s, especially, widen the design of the detective formula to include the background of society and the relationships among its inhabitants.

She believed that if detective fiction was to survive "it *must* get back to where it began in the hands of Collins and LeFanu, and become once more a novel of manners instead of a pure crossword puzzle." Collins was a better model for her than Poe because Collins added the dimension of living char-

acters and social values to the crafted puzzle and careful design of Poe's
dreamlike creations.

Looking back on her career, Sayers admitted that in the early twenties,
she began to write blithely with the aim to construct detective novels that
were closer to novels of manners and character than to intellectual puzzles.
She found, however, that "one cannot write a novel unless one has something
to say about life" and that she could say nothing because she knew nothing.

First she had to learn how to tell a detective story. One of her earliest
concerns was how to unify her novels. In 1928, she indicated the difficulty of
including more than the intellectual puzzle and still retaining a unified design. The further the detective story "escapes from pure analysis, the more
difficulty it has in achieving artistic unity." The further the story departs
from the puzzle-solution formula, the less pure it is as a detective story. But
it had to escape if it was to achieve what Dorothy Sayers hoped for the genre.

A detective-fiction writer was caught between the puzzle and the characters: "A too violent emotion flung into the glittering mechanism of the
detective-story jars the movement by disturbing its delicate balance." In her
novels of the 1920s, Sayers oiled and polished the glittering machinery of the
detective story, but she could not resist testing its balance also.

In the late twenties, she expressed a popular belief that the detective
novel "does not, and by hypothesis never can, attain the loftiest level of
literary achievement," a belief that she challenged. By 1930 she could say
that "within the necessary restrictions of its form, it is as capable of its own
proper greatness as a sonnet within the restrictions of octave and sestet."
During the twenties, she improved her ability to handle the restrictions of the
detective story as she explored the possibilities of its design in order to find
its level of literary achievement.

One of the restrictions of the detective story results from the conventional puzzle. The reader expects to be entertained by a merry chase. Using a
playful analogy, Sayers described the detective writer's ideal reader as "an
intelligent terrier, ears cocked and tail wagging, ready to run after what is
thrown to him and to root cheerfully among the shrubbery till he finds it."

Sayers's early novels were written in the spirit of throwing a ball to a
happy, cheerful terrier. In such later novels of the 1930s as *The Documents
in the Case, Gaudy Night,* and *Busman's Honeymoon,* we may root in the
shrubbery, but the ball thrown inspires more reflection than eagerness. Even
as early as *Whose Body?* (1923), the design of her novels asks a little more of
us than wagging tails. For the most part, however, that first novel concentrates on appealing to our love of a good guessing game.

When *Whose Body?* was published, *The Nation* called it "the maddest, jolliest crime story of recent memory." Its beginning is outrageous. A nervous, timid architect, Mr. Thipps, finds a corpse in his bathtub. The man has been shaved, perfumed, and laid neatly in the tub. He is nude except for a gold pair of pince-nez.

Lord Peter is called in to investigate because his mother knows Mr. Thipps. Meanwhile, Wimsey's friend, Inspector Charles Parker of Scotland Yard (who will be promoted to Chief Inspector in *The Unpleasantness at the Bellona Club*) has begun another case, the disappearance of the wealthy financier Sir Reuben Levy. Inspector Sugg (whose retirement is announced in *The Nine Tailors*) thinks that the nude body and Levy's are the same. Having seen the corpse, Peter affirms that it cannot be Levy's, that the idea is preposterous. Tactfully for Sayers's audience, Peter means that the body has not been circumcised; therefore, it cannot be the Orthodox Jewish financier's.

The novel begins, then, intriguingly focuses on a body with a missing identity and an identity with a missing body. Gradually Lord Peter discovers that the two mysteries are related, but not in the way Sugg hypothesized.

In *Whose Body?* Sayers constructs a fair puzzle. We see the murderer early; Peter knows who he is in Chapter VIII. We know for certain in Chapter XI, the penultimate chapter of the book.

To solve the puzzle, this first novel relies on busy-work and lengthy speculations. We learn about the Levy household as our attention is directed to the actions of Wimsey's valet, Bunter, who sets up an enormous camera. He uncorks a bottle of gray powder, sprinkles it around, adjusts arc-lights, and takes photographs of fingerprints.

The photographs disclose a scarred thumb print and another print superimposed upon it. Wimsey also finds a significant hair in Levy's bedroom. His conclusion: two sets of prints, two kinds of hair. Someone's been sleeping in Sir Reuben's bed.

Besides the busy-work, talk advances the plot—slowly. Lord Peter and Charles speculate about the pince-nez; Lord Peter and his mother talk about the absurdity of Mr. Thipps's arrest. We listen to the detailed enumeration of the fingerprints that Bunter photographs and Wimsey's divisions and subdivisions of Hypotheses 1 and 2 and Alternatives A and B. By now, several readers may have decided to skip pages until the ball rolls down the hill. Even in a jolly novel, one can become as bogged down as Lord Peter in *Clouds of Witness* (1926), Sayers's second novel.

When Gerald chides Peter for being a wastrel, *Whose Body?* anticipates the plot of *Clouds of Witness*. Peter replies in the first novel, "I'm bein' no end useful. You may come to want me yourself, you never know. When somebody comes blackmailin' you, Gerald . . . you'll realize the pull of havin' a private detective in the family."

In the second novel, during a house party at Riddlesdale Lodge in Yorkshire, Gerald Wimsey, the Duke of Denver, discovers the body of Denis Cathcart, his sister Mary's fiancé. He cannot—or will not—explain why he was outside at 3:00 A.M. After hearing testimony at the inquest, the jury concludes that Gerald ought to be tried for willful murder.

Neither Charles Parker nor Peter Wimsey, nor the reader for that matter, believes Gerald to be guilty. Lord Peter determines to answer two questions and prove his brother's innocence: how did Cathcart die and where was Gerald Wimsey?

Like *Whose Body?*, *Clouds of Witness* keeps readers and characters busy chasing clues. Peter and Charles follow several leads—a diamond pin, Cathcart's account books, the inhabitants at the Grimethorpe farm, Lady Mary's activities with the Soviet Club. In fact, Lady Mary appears to be guilty when Bunter finds suspicious bloodstains on her skirt and when, in her clothes chest, Lord Peter finds silver sand from the scene of Cathcart's death. Enamored of Mary, Charles defends her. (He becomes engaged to Mary in *Strong Poison*; we find they have married and have two children in *Murder Must Advertise*).

To intrigue the reader, Sayers introduces the Person Unknown for Charles and Peter to trail. Together they follow evidence down the path that leads from the house and the conservatory through a little wood in the park fence. The trail leads to the belt of a burberry coat and the toeprints of Unknown where he went over the tall pickets.

Their dialogue lifts the reader's nose out of the gravel and demonstrates why many speak of Sayers's sleuthing devices as jolly. We hear one example of their dialogue in *Whose Body?* When he detects the significant hair, Peter bends over the pillow and tries not to breathe too hard for fear of losing the important clue. He asks Parker to give him the tweezers. Then he angrily cautions, "Good heavens, man, don't blow like that, you might be a whale." In *Clouds of Witness*, with Peter on his shoulders, Parker grumbles that he wishes Peter would drop off because he's breaking Parker's collarbone.

The David and Jonathan relationship of Lord Peter and Charles Parker continues throughout their literary lives, but never more humorously than in the early novels. The comic mixture of Charles's petulance and Peter's exuberance relieves the monotony of pursuing the necessary clues.

In following the trail from the conservatory, Charles and Peter re-enact the movements of the Person Unknown. Peter: "Here he is, on a squashed fungus." Charles: "This broken branch may be our friend—I think it is." Peter: "I've lost him altogether." Charles: "He's tripped over a root." Besides being entertainment for the reader, the device of making the unseen visible is central to the novel.

Wimsey stops his search temporarily in Chapter XII when, in a thick fog, he steps into a dangerous, sucking bog. Bunter drives a walking stick into the ground. Then he ties a string around the stick and inches forward, "clue in hand," to aid his master. They see a light approaching. Shouting, they tell the rescuers to follow the string. The rescuers pull Lord Peter from the mire and take him to Grider's Hole, the Grimethorpe farm. There, he finds Gerald's alibi. The scene advances the plot; it also suggests one theme of the novel, which is concerned with appearances that obscure the truth.

At the beginning of *Clouds of Witness*, to Peter "the world presented itself as an entertaining labyrinth of side-issues." Like the bog, however, the labyrinth leads to related issues (the Grimethorpe farm, *Manon Lescaut*). The answers to the two questions, of who killed Denis Cathcart and where was Gerald Wimsey the night Cathcart died are related. Along with the mechanics of detecting, the puzzle in *Clouds of Witness* presents a human puzzle that anticipates *The Documents in the Case* (1930).

As a detective-fiction reader herself, Sayers knew that her readers expected a playful, tantalizing, and fair chase. She also knew that repeating the game too exactly endangers its longevity. The more a reader learns about the methods of a particular author, the less effective the writer may seem. "The mystery-monger's principal difficulty," she acknowledged, "is that of varying his surprises."

To vary the mechanics of detection, Sayers created entertaining characters and moved the detective out of the armchair. To vary her surprises, she asked different questions. She concluded that "of the three questions, Who? How? and Why? How? is at present [1928] the one which offers most scope for surprise and ingenuity and is capable of sustaining an entire book on its own, though a combination of all three naturally provides the best entertainment."

She could be describing her own progression. Her first two novels ask Who? and *Unnatural Death* (American title: *The Dawson Pedigree*, 1927) asks How? Not until *The Nine Tailors* (1934) will the method of death lead us on as complex a chase as *Unnatural Death*.

Miss Agatha Dawson, stricken with terminal cancer, dies earlier than her doctor had predicted. In a restaurant, Dr. Carr happens to overhear Lord Peter remark to Charles Parker that doctors have no business "thinking." They can get into trouble. Dr. Carr excuses himself and enters the discussion with his story.

The wealthy Miss Dawson was in her seventies. Her niece, in her mid-twenties, and a nurse had taken care of her. The combination of cancer and old age would have carried her off, but something odd happened. When Dr. Carr saw her in November 1925, he affirmed that she would live another five or six months. Three days later, however, she was dead.

The doctor had performed an autopsy and found nothing. Still dissatisfied, he made an analysis and found nothing. Against his professional judgment, he signed the certificate that attributed Miss Dawson's death to natural causes. The body was buried without an inquest. The doctor's delay, however, caused a scandal. The body was not cremated as planned. Now the doctor has lost his patients and regrets that he ever tried to be a conscientious citizen. He agrees with Wimsey that doctors should not go about "thinking" things.

The story arouses Lord Peter's interest. He qualifies his imperative. Doctors, or anyone, can get into trouble for thinking things aloud without supporting them with a spark of evidence. By Chapter III, Lord Peter suspects the murderer; his suspicions are shared by Nurse Philliter and by the reader. In Chapter V, that important and colorful addition to Wimsey detection, Miss Alexandra Katherine Climpson, adds one more vote. From then on, Wimsey does not rest until he has a bonfire of real evidence. It takes the cautious Charles longer. In Chapter XIV, he agrees that possibly Agatha Dawson's death was murder, for in that chapter Lord Peter finds the motive. Thereafter with the questions Who? and Why? answered, only How? remains.

Throughout the game Sayers plays fair. She presents a subtle clue in Chapter II ("And nothing came of it?"); in Chapter VII Lord Peter looks right at the whole metaphorical ball. The cyclist in Chapter XI may seem to be arbitrary, but he, too, belongs in the trail. As Miss Climpson leaves church she finds an important scrap of paper with penitent confessional notes. If Sayers has to rely on a *deus ex machina*, what better place than a church?

Fair play and unity of action distinguish this novel and vary its surprise. To interlock the parts, Sayers uses the very essence of the drama of detection —dissembling. All of the major characters dissemble at least once; some, twice or more. In seeking answers to the death of Bertha Gotobed, one of

Miss Dawson's former employees, Lord Peter and Parker visit Mrs. Forrest. Peter assumes the name of Mr. Templeton. Getting into his role, Wimsey trots out of the room and clumsily clatters around in the kitchen where Mrs. Forrest cannot see him. Parker meanwhile fidgets with embarrassment for he does not recognize that Wimsey is acting in order to search for more clues. Later, Wimsey becomes Mr. Simms-Gaythorpe so that, under the camouflage of gossip, he can question the nurse that replaced Miss Philliter.

Miss Climpson uses the disguise of a comfortably wealthy, retired lady in order to take up residence near the Dawson home. As Lord Peter instructs, she is to find out all that she can; her skill in gossip allows her to succeed.

Through her, even conservative Charles Parker dissembles. Miss Climpson introduces him to her landlady as her nephew Adolphus so that Mrs. Budge will not suspect an official visit. On his own, Parker fibs·about why he wants to know about the new inheritance law from a lawyer.

Miss Dawson's niece, Mary Whittaker, also discovers the significance of the new inheritance law when she is in disguise. As Miss Grant, she calls on a Bloomsbury solicitor, Mr. Tigg. When he sees her later, she says that her name is Mrs. Marion Mead.

With our ears cocked and our tails wagging, we watch the ball disappear behind the shrubs more than once. The feints and disguises keep us going. They also effect a pervasively unnatural atmosphere and thus become more than just an ingenious mechanism. The disguises that are necessary to the puzzle are also integral elements in the overall design of *Unnatural Death*.

In Sayers's fourth novel, *The Unpleasantness at the Bellona Club* (1928), the puzzle mechanism runs more smoothly than in any of her previous works. Not only had she learned the craft of presenting a puzzle, clues, and solution, she also had taught her readers how to read her novels. To her, fair play meant that she would not mention characters or objects unless she planned to use them later. When Mr. Murbles explains to Lord Peter that the question about General Fentiman's death involves a will, we know that the document will be central to the puzzle and a key to the "unpleasantness" in the title. When a telephone booth is mentioned several times, we can be alert to its importance also.

The story begins on the morning of November 11 when ninety-year-old General Fentiman is discovered dead in his chair at the Bellona Club. His wealthy sister, Felicity Dormer, died at 10:37 the same morning. The General's usual hour for arriving at the Club was 10:00; however, no one had seen him arrive on the morning of the 11th.

At first, the novel asks one question: at what precise time did the General die? The precise time of his death is important because of his sister's will. It stipulates that, besides £12,000 to her ward, Ann Dorland, the remainder of her fortune is to go to the General *if* he was still alive at her death. If not, Ann Dorland would inherit the bulk of the fortune and £15,000 was to be divided equally between the General's grandsons, Robert and George Fentiman.

To tighten the screw, the General also left a will. To George Fentiman, the younger grandson, he left all of his securities, a small legacy, but all that he had. He explained that George's need was greater than that of his older brother, Robert. To Robert, the General left any other monies, which meant that Robert could inherit the Dormer fortune.

Compared with Sayers's previous novels, the search for answers in *Bellona Club* is a relaxed affair. Most of the frenetic busy-ness of the first two novels and most of the will'o-the-wisps of the third have disappeared. Bunter takes only a few photographs. In fact, Bunter almost disappears in this novel except to bring Wimsey changes of clothes—silently.

Beginning with the discovery of the General's body, the novel proceeds in a leisurely manner. In Chapter I, Sayers uses understatement as though she no longer fears losing her reader. Returning from General Fentiman's chair, for example, Colonel Marchbanks (a long-time member of the Club) walks over to Lord Peter, "I say, Peter, just come over here a moment. I'm afraid something rather unpleasant has happened." Cooly, Sayers slips an important clue into Chapter II when the narrator announces that no one remembered speaking with the General that morning. She waits until Chapter III to let us know that we are in for some problem solving, as Mr. Murbles tells Lord Peter that "a curious question has arisen with regard to the sad death of General Fentiman at the Bellona Club"—the question about the precise moment of death.

Questions become more curious when, as late as Chapter XIV, the characters learn inadvertently that the General's death was murder. Not only are we to answer the question when did he die, but also, this late in the novel, who killed him and how? To wait so long to introduce the crime into her detective novel not only varies the surprise, it also demonstrates Sayers's increased confidence in her craft.

For example, in her earlier novels, she seemed to have been uneasy about how to present her data. Either her characters must be in a room speculating about the evidence (*Whose Body?* and *Clouds of Witness*), listening to testimony (*Clouds of Witness*), or listening to local inhabitants' stories in dialect (*Clouds of Witness* and *Unnatural Death*). Her fourth novel delivers clues more subtly.

We can compare two incidents about a blotting pad, one in *Clouds*, the other in *Bellona Club*. In the former, Lord Peter

> slipped a paper-knife under the top sheet of the blotting-pad and held it up to the light. "Quite right, old man. Give you full marks for observation. Here's Jerry's signature, and the Colonel's and a long sprawly hand, which I should judge to be feminine." He looked at the sheet again, shook his head, folded it up, and placed it in his pocketbook. "Doesn't seem to be anything there," he commented, "but you never know."

We can compare the above with the crispness of a similar scene in *Bellona Club*:

> Wimsey took up the blotting-pad to blot his notes. Then his face changed. The corner of a sheet of paper protruded slightly. On the principle that nothing is too small to be looked at, Wimsey poked an inquisitive finger between the leaves, and extracted the paper.

In both incidents, Wimsey finds important clues. From the earlier *Clouds* to *Bellona Club*, however, Sayers discovered how to use her narrator to render the actions.

In her 1928 introduction to the first series of short stories that she edited, Sayers examined E. C. Bentley's manipulation of points of view in *Trent's Last Case*. The analysis seems to have benefited her own writing. As in all of her novels, dialogue carries much of the story in *Bellona Club*, but the intercession of the narrator varies and relaxes the pace, as in the passage above. In her earlier novels, one has the impression of watching a vaudeville comic changing hats and voices for fear of boring the audience. By *Bellona Club*, one hears a novelist's confident narration.

Sayers's narrator describes material integral to the puzzle, such as Peter's search that reveals an important clue, and the discovery of General Fentiman's death, which initiates the puzzle. The latter is set against the social background of the conservative Bellona Club. The narrator explains the attitudes of its members. "It is doubtful which occurrence was more disagreeable to the senior members of the Bellona Club—the grotesque death of General Fentiman in their midst or the indecent neurasthenia of his grandson." When Lord Peter picks up General Fentiman's body, frozen in a sitting position, his grandson George laughs hysterically over the fact that his grandfather had been dead for two days and no one realized it. He shouts that they are all dead and no one has noticed that either. "Only the younger men felt no sense of outrage; they knew too much," says the narrator. The older men euphemistically classify the disruption of the Club's pacific decorum as an unpleasantness. Because of the war, the younger men knew too much about death and its effects on the living to feel outraged by either.

"Unpleasantness" in the novel's title pinpoints the attitude of the older Bellona Club's members toward any breach of decorum, including someone's death in their serene midst. Their reactions to the General's death satirize those who worship traditions that have become dead forms.

Robert Fentiman disdainfully speaks about "those refrigerated old imbeciles at the Club sittin' solemnly round there, and comin' in and noddin' to the old gov'nor like so many mandarins, when he was dead as a door-nail all the time." (In *Have His Carcase*, 1932, the decorum of clubs still represents a source of death-in-life to Sayers, as illustrated when Peter pleads with Harriet, "Call me anything you like, but not dreary! Not one of those things you find in clubs!")

To Sayers, structure is essential in life as well as in art, but when it hardens like Poe's Prefect's procrustean methods, it loses its vitality. Rigidly imitating the analytical tradition of the detective short story, for example, would mean certain death for detective fiction, in her opinion. To restore the vitality of what she already considered to be a frozen carcass, Sayers tested those restrictions of the detective novel.

To detect clues and deduce significant relationships, the detective first dissects the puzzle and then reconstructs the resulting data. In order to avoid detection, the criminal dons masks by dissembling and plays a game of hide and seek. The design of each of Sayers's first four novels evolves from one of these actions central to the art of detection: dissection in *Whose Body?*; reconstruction in *Clouds of Witness*; disguise in *Unnatural Death*, and gaming in *The Unpleasantness at the Bellona Club*. In these four novels, the mechanics of the genre glitter with life and artistic seriousness.

The first chapter of *Whose Body?* mentions the dissecting room; the last chapter returns to it. Meanwhile, Lord Peter dissects the problem of the missing and the found bodies. By examining parts—the hair, the fingerprints, Sir Reuben Levy's activities the night he disappeared, his diary—Wimsey recreates the whole and solves the puzzle. What begins as comedy and detached armchair speculation ends with the grisly revelation of Levy's having been literally dissected by the renowned medical specialist and researcher, Sir Julian Freke.

Freke is one of Sayers's most evil characters. As a result of the base emotion jealousy, he not only murders and defiles a kindly, affectionate man, he flaunts and misuses his medical skill. Freke kills without conscience, for he believes that "the knowledge of good and evil is an observed phenomenon, attendant upon a certain condition of the brain-cells, which is removable."

Although Lord Peter cannot restore Levy to his family, he can balance the murderer's dissection. Unlike Freke, who uses his skill to destroy harmony, Wimsey uses his powers of dissection to restore it. Confronted, the murderer admits defeat by Wimsey's synthesis.

The next novel, *Clouds of Witness*, also dramatizes an action that one recognizes as characteristic of the art of detection—reconstruction. The Coroner reconstructs the story of October 13 and 14 from separate testimonies at the inquest in the first chapter; Charles Parker and Peter Wimsey reconstruct, even relive, the activities of the night of October 13 by following signs on the floor of the conservatory and down the path to the park. In his summation speech, Sir Impey Biggs tells the jury of Lords that in order to untangle the threads of Cathcart's story, he will begin at the beginning. He reconstructs Cathcart's life from his birth to his death, including the moments of his dying, in inimitable Sir Impey style, which includes the death throes.

Wimsey's dramatic open-cockpit flight from America brings facts that free Gerald, but Sir Impey's drama enlivens the plain facts and shares Cathcart's experiences with the listener, just as Peter's and Charles's drama brings the events of October 13 to life. "Damn it all," Peter stresses, "we want to get at the truth!" The legal structures facilitate the action once the events of Cathcart's story are known; the artistic structure of Sir Impey's presentation, in which a dead man speaks, presents the truth of Cathcart's experience.

The artistic design of the novel tells us even more. In a comic interlude at the Soviet Club, Lord Peter overhears a lunchroom conversation about the structure of modern art. One speaker lauds James Joyce for freeing writers from "the superstition of syntax." Another suggests that expression needs a new notational system, a system that better represents human emotion. This chapter is followed by Charles's methodical use of the conventional notational system to record Lady Mary's story.

To learn the story of Cathcart and the events of his death, we must follow the sequence of the novel like Peter's rescuers follow a string through the fog. In addition to the evidence presented at the inquest in Chapter 1, the story depends upon information that Charles and Peter find, one of the most

important pieces being the novel *Manon Lescaut*. It is not introduced as legal
evidence until Sir Impey's summation at Gerald's trial in the House of Lords,
when he compares Cathcart to the main character of *Manon*. Although we
must consider the legal evidence to find out what happened in the early
morning of October 14, artistic evidence, finally, will allow us a glimpse of
the truth of Denis Cathcart's emotions, their depth and their part in his
death.

In addition to the plot's sequential reconstruction of events, the relationship among the three principal characters allows us to reconstruct a
larger design than the story of one man's death. For example, *Clouds of
Witness* begins with Lord Peter's return from a three-month vacation in Cor-
sica, "admiring at a cautious distance the wild beauty of Corsican peasant-
women, and studying the vendetta in its natural haunt." Before he returns to
London, however, he visits Paris to heed his sexuality, the "call of the
blood."

The beginning of the novel thus establishes a basic relationship among
Peter Wimsey, Denis Cathcart, and Gerald Wimsey, whose own story is
entangled with that of Mr. Grimethorpe. The novel ends not with Gerald's
trial, but after the trial and after the desperate Mr. Grimethorpe, jealous of
his exotically beautiful wife's sexual relationship with Gerald, tries to kill
Gerald and is himself killed. Through what may seem to be side issues to the
Cathcart story twine the threads of *Manon Lescaut*, whose tragic tale of sex
and love deepens the story Sir Impey tells about Cathcart.

We infer that Cathcart identified with Abbé Prévost's story about the
Chevalier des Grieux, who loved a faithless harlot so intensely that he gave
up family and friends for her. From our own and Sir Impey's inferences, we
learn that Denis Cathcart's actions fit into the universal pattern of human
craving—the "call of the blood"—Lord Peter's, Gerald Wimsey's, Mr.
Grimethorpe's.

Denis Cathcart kept the novel, *Manon Lescaut*, in his room at the
Riddlesdale Lodge. Appropriately, Peter is in Cathcart's room when he tells
Parker that he did not keep up with his sister Mary's engagement to Cathcart
because after he got "the chuck" from his girlfriend, Barbara, he did not feel
like bothering with others' romances.

The Prévost novel gives Wimsey the clue that saves his brother. It gives
us the clue to Cathcart's passion and his death. In Chapter V, Parker examines Cathcart's Paris apartment, where he finds Cathcart's account books and
photograph. We follow those signs to reconstruct the economic life of Denis
Cathcart, who withdrew large sums of money in December 1919. Later, we

see the inter-relatedness of that fact, the sensuality manifest in Cathcart's photograph, and *Manon Lescaut*.

After *Clouds of Witness* answers the puzzles about Who? and How? it suggests a much more complex human puzzle about Denis Cathcart than merely how he met his death. It also suggests that the detective genre can show us that the plain facts belong in the court, but that art structures a truth that reaches beyond the certainties of admissible evidence. Just as Lord Peter, Charles, and Sir Impey reconstruct actions from the signs that they follow, so the reader can reconstruct their significance by following the larger design of the novel.

One of the difficulties of the detective genre, claims Chesterton, derives from its having to wait until the very end to tell us "the most interesting things about the most interesting people." In *Clouds of Witness*, by means of *Manon Lescaut*, however, Sayers has been showing us a most interesting clue to Cathcart's death all along.

In *Unnatural Death* her sleights of hand also challenge the restrictions of the genre as they become part of the structure of the novel. Detective fiction, by nature, must be "a drama of masks and not of faces. It depends on man's false characters rather than their real characters. . . . It is a masquerade ball in which everyone is disguised as everybody else. . . ." As though to take Chesterton to a literal extreme, Sayers puts all of her major characters in masks in *Unnatural Death*.

The masquerades vary the surprises and keep the reader interested in the puzzle of how Miss Dawson died (we know early who killed her). Even more significantly, the disguises contribute to the plot's design by heightening the atmosphere of unnaturalness that surrounds the death and the murderer.

As in *Whose Body?* we are to consider the ethics of the murder; although Miss Dawson was old and dying, she wanted to live. By killing her, Mary Whittaker kills a generous, kindly relative. Like Freke in *Whose Body?*, Mary Whittaker of *Unnatural Death* misuses her reason and violates the family. To suggest that these actions are perversions of human nature, Sayers chooses the motif of unnaturalness.

The masks and disguises that may restrict the writer of detective fiction not only advance Sayers's story in *Unnatural Death*, but also suggest the quality of evil. Mary Whittaker dissembles. She is an artificer who disguises rather than reveals, who destroys rather than creates. As if to emphasize the negative quality of her influence, Chapter XII, in the middle of the novel, presents a pastoral, fertile contrast—the country town of Crofton, which remains untouched by the sterility of spirit that characterizes Mary Whittaker. In this chapter, Mrs. Cobling enumerates her progeny—five children, fourteen grandchildren, three great-grandchildren. The sheets of the inn smell of lavender. In a courtyard, Peter watches ducks, a spaniel, a cat as they enjoy themselves in the bright morning sun. The barman hospitably opens the door of the inn to admit Peter.

By contrast, the city of London—"the repository of so many odd secrets. Discreet, incurious and all-enfolding London"—represents an extension of Mary Whittaker. There, as Mr. Templeton, Lord Peter calls on Mrs. Forrest. Although she wears an exotic costume like out of the *Arabian Nights*, when she tries to seduce him, she arouses no call of the blood. So grim, so awkward, so unnatural is her attempt that he doubts her story about fearing that her husband will catch her with her lover (Chapter XV). Dressed in a fantastic turban of gold tissue, Mrs. Forrest disguises an odd secret, her relationship to Mary Whittaker.

When she first meets Miss Whittaker, Miss Climpson recognizes her "frustrated womanhood." It is not a frustration born of eagerness "to mate before youth could depart." From experience, Miss Climpson knows that frustration; she has seen it on her own face. Unlike Miss Whittaker, however, Miss Climpson, "was a spinster made and not born—a perfectly womanly woman." The latter belongs in the natural order but has been frustrated by society; the former, who denies her sexuality, is unnatural. One is unfortunate; the other, dangerous.

In *Unnatural Death*, fertility, naturalness, hospitality, and a sharing of the self are equated with goodness; sterility, unnaturalness, closing off the self in disguises are equated with evil. Mary Whittaker's implicit lesbianism (Sayers never uses the word), like the disguises in the novel, is a literary device to evaluate the murderer. Sayers does not seem to be condemning lesbians or women who choose to live without men.

Agatha Dawson and Clara Whittaker, a beautiful and high-spirited woman, lived together for many years. Similar to Miss Findlater's telling Miss Climpson that she and Mary Whittaker intend to live together without men and be happy, Agatha Dawson had told Mrs. Cobling years before that she and Miss Clara intended "to live together and be ever so happy, without any stupid, tiresome gentlemen." They may have been lesbians; we shall never know. What their roles in the novel suggest is that they are contrasts to Mary Whittaker.

She is dishonest and greedy, misusing her own humanity as well as others'. Wimsey pronounces her rapacious; even kindly Miss Climpson calls her a "beastly, blood-sucking woman." Beyond these explicit comments, the masks that characterize the detective genre allow Sayers in *Unnatural Death* an unexpected means of presenting the puzzle and solution of a crime but also of emphasizing evil as anti-nature, as represented by the murderer.

The plot of *The Unpleasantness at the Bellona Club* also depends upon an action central to the conventions of detective fiction—the art of gaming, Robert Fentiman plays a game using Mr. Oliver to fool Lord Peter; Lord Peter in turn matches wits with Robert with an equally engaging game. The chapter titles compare the progression of the story to a card game: "Lord Peter Leads Through Strength" and "Lord Peter Forces a Card." These games suggest another more serious game, the effects of which pervade the community in this novel—war.

While the Great War physically handicapped Captain Culyer, the Secretary of the Bellona Club, it mentally impaired George Fentiman. His condition then affects his ability to hold a job; his not being able to work in turn strains his relationship with his wife, who must find work.

He tells his wife that it is her place to speak to the servants. Then he tries to carry the coal for her. Sheila accuses him of being chivalrous suddenly because Peter is visiting them. She has been carrying more than coal, of course. She works because he cannot, yet he blames women: "No wonder a man can't get a decent job these days with these hard-mouthed, cigarette-smoking females all over the place, pretending they're geniuses and business women and all the rest of it." He complains that in the old days women hired out as companions, that the modern woman thinks only of money, that she has no "decent feeling or sentiment about her." Finally, George apologizes to Lord Peter (but not to his wife) for his "rotten bad form."

The rules of what George refers to as form and decency changed because of the war, as did relationships between women and men, a subject that continues in the rest of Sayers's novels. All forms are different after the war. One cannot even be certain of traditional behavior during the Armistice Day two-minute silence. When Mr. Murbles finds out that part of Robert Fentiman's game—hiding the General's body—began during the silence, he expresses his horror: "God bless my soul! How abominable! How—how blasphemous! Really, I cannot find words. This is the most disgraceful thing I ever heard of."

The younger men who have returned from World War I feel no sense of outrage at such trifles. George Fentiman tells Wimsey that unlike the Crimean War of his grandfather, World War I was a *real* war. He criticizes his grandfather for thinking that "things can go on just as they did half a century ago," but even George and Mr. Murbles are learning what change does to a society. The forms of social behavior and relationships are all changing— and so, for that matter, is art.

The books in Ann Dorland's room include authors who were known for their experiments with new content and forms—Dorothy Richardson, Virginia Woolf, D. H. Lawrence. Music changed also. Wimsey sits at the piano to play. He has just informed Murbles that he will research the General's death if Murbles promises to accept whatever he finds. Speaking for his times, he advises the solicitor to adopt a detached view of life. As Wimsey sits at the piano in this detached frame of mind, he discards Bach. After his fingers form a crooning melody by the composer Parry, he laughs and plays "an odd, noisy, and painfully inharmonious study by a modern composer in the key of seven sharps."

New, often discordant, art forms manifest the painful detachment of the 1920s. Sayers recognized that the detective novel had a place in this postwar era. She speculated that among other literatures of escape, "the cheerful cynicism of the detective-tale suits better with the spirit of the times than the sentimentality which ends in wedding bells."

Lord Peter tells Ann Dorland that while he was hospitalized, he "only played one game, the very simplest . . . the demon . . . a silly game with no ideas in it at all. I just went on laying it out and gathering it up . . . hundred times in an evening . . . so as to stop thinking." He said that he also read detective stories to stop thinking because all the other books had either love or war in them.

The kind of detective fiction that Lord Peter read in 1918 was not the kind that Dorothy Sayers wrote in the 1920s, silly games with no ideas in them. As fair games that entertain, her first novels demonstrate a thoughtful craftsman at work, one who is exploring the limits of the genre. By constructing the novels to emphasize the materials of the art of detection, Sayers not only subtly comments on the murderer (*Whose Body?* and *Unnatural Death*), the victim (*Clouds of Witness*), and society (*The Unpleasantness at the Bellona Club*), she also implicitly comments on the nature of the genre.

Her first novels show that the actions of the detective—dissection and reconstruction—and of the criminal—disguise and gaming—not only fulfill the mechanical conventions of detective fiction. They can also become rich ingredients in a complex design.

Detective fiction need not be thrills with no shape. It need not sacrifice humanity to the puzzle. Her last novel of the 1920s, *The Unpleasantness at the Bellona Club*, anticipates the delicate balance that Sayers most often strove to maintain, a balance between manners and puzzles. In the 1930s she continued to construct unified designs of interlocking parts. She thickened their textures by including living characters and a recognizable and representative society.

3

TOWARD A DETECTIVE NOVEL OF MANNERS

The Documents in the Case
Strong Poison

In "The Present Status of the Mystery Story," which appeared in *The London Mercury* in November 1930, Sayers describes what she regarded as a crisis for detective fiction: "It is in great danger of losing touch with the common man, and becoming a caviare banquet for the cultured." Instead of being read by everyone, detective stories were read only by scientists, artists, and clergymen. Sayers was disturbed that well-written books like Bentley's *Trent's Last Case* and Chesterton's Father Brown stories were being ignored because the readers had begun to associate detective fiction with problem-solving only, fiction that had nothing to say about common human feelings and conditions. Detective fiction was "in some danger of having the marrow squeezed out of it."

To Sayers, the marrow of detective fiction, like that of any story of lasting importance, depended upon its appeal to the reader's sensations, to his interest and emotions. Contrary to the bad legacy of sensationalism—thrills without shape, Sayers believed that at its best, which means in a unified design, sensational appeal creates an awareness of a reality other than the familiar, unquestioned world, and also an understanding of common human feelings. Wilkie Collins's ability to evoke mysterious and inexplicable happenings as well as passionate and basic human feelings, all within a work structured as carefully as a classical drama, led Sayers to prefer him as a model for the detective form over Poe. She criticized those imitators of Poe who, unlike Collins, forgot that the detective novel ought to be more than a long puzzle. She criticized them for polishing the machinery only, for sacrificing humanity to gadgetry.

By November 1930, when she diagnosed what she considered to be the failing health of detective fiction, she had already begun to improve it. *The Documents in the Case* (July 1930) and *Strong Poison* (September 1930) indicate the directions her novels were to continue to follow in order to restore life and color to the genre.

In *The Documents in the Case* she concentrated on the people in one household to show how they were affected by the social values of a post-war suburban society. She presented manners as well as a murder mystery, but as though to test what she could do without him, Sayers eliminated Lord Peter. In *The Development of the Detective Novel*, A. E. Murch says, "Technically, the novel is superb, but it lacks the stimulating presence of Lord Peter Wimsey. . . ." Murch's coordinating conjunction implies that without Lord Peter the novel falters. Actually, his absence gives the novel its power and gave Sayers a way to write a novel of manners without having to conform to her readers' expectations about Peter Wimsey's behavior or guidance. Looking back after seven years, Sayers claimed that "*The Documents in the Case,* which is a serious 'criticism of life' so far as it goes, took a jump forward rather out of its due time." That it took a jump forward may be one reason that it remains one of her most intriguing novels in form and in content.

The book is a collection of letters and official documents that gradually reconstruct the events that lead to the death of George Harrison and to the conviction and execution of his murderer. Without the familiar detective, the readers are on their own to piece together the story of the suburban couple, George and Margaret Harrison. At age 56, Mr. Harrison has a respectable job as head of the accounts department of an electrical engineering firm. His second wife, Margaret, is much younger than he. They are childless. Paul, Mr. Harrison's son by his first marriage, works as a civil engineer in Africa. After his father's death, he returns to England where he collects and collates the documents to make a case about his father's death.

Apparently, Mr. Harrison died by accidentally eating a poisoned toadstool. His son does not accept the verdict of death by accident. His father's avocation, which was cooking with native fungi and unusual wildlife—including hedgehog—had produced a cookbook, *Neglected Edible Treasures.* He had tested all of the recipes and had illustrated the book after carefully researching each item. He ought to have been able to distinguish the poisonous from the nonpoisonous mushroom, concludes his son.

The documents he collects include letters from the housekeeper, Miss Agatha Milsom, and two boarders—an artist, Harwood Lathom, and a novelist, John Munting. The use of letters as an expository device in a narrative is not new. Wilkie Collins used it in *The Moonstone* (1868), Bram Stoker, in *Dracula* (1891), and it goes back further to the eighteenth-century epistolary novels of Samuel Richardson. For the detective novel, the epistolary form is particularly appropriate. The reader actively must detect clues from among the documents.

In *The Documents in the Case* the reader not only is guided by the chronology to examine the causal relationships of the novel's actions, he also begins to examine psychological and social relationships of the characters. The novel focuses on the relationship between Margaret and her husband. Each correspondent sees the Harrisons a bit differently, a technique that dramatizes the complexity of the human personality and the danger of making facile judgments. In *The Mind of the Maker*, written several years after her last detective novel, Sayers cautioned against the simplistic assumption

> that all human situations are "problems" like detective problems, capable of a single, necessary, and categorical solution, which must be wholly right, while all others are wholly wrong. But this they cannot be, since human situations are subject to the law of human nature, whose evil is at all times rooted in its good, and whose good can only redeem, but not abolish, its evil.

In the relationship of George and Margaret Harrison, who can say which of them was more evil than good?

Several characters observe Margaret Harrison and reach conclusions that together present a portrait of her. Paul Harrison, who never liked his young stepmother, suspects her of hypocrisy. Her gushing manner and mourning apparel after his father's death nauseate him. According to Agatha Milsom, whose inferences may be governed by her own problems of repression, Mrs. Harrison is an impractical dreamer, but vibrant and eager to please. The novelist Munting, whose voice is the most authoritative in the novel, characterizes Margaret Harrison as "a sort of suburban vamp, an ex-typist or something, and entirely wrapped up, I should say, in her own attractions." As a writer, he admits that she interests him as a type—not harmful, but amoral. He judges her merely as silly. Yet her silliness, egotism, and dreaming lead to the death of her husband.

And what of the victim? Again John Munting, ever observant, renders him for the reader. Harrison is nice enough, even likeable. His penchant for exactness becomes tedious, however, especially when he interrupts Munting's work to discuss grammatical accuracy.

About Harrison's relationship with his wife, Munting speculates, "I fancy he must have read somewhere that women like to be treated rough and feel the tight hand on the rein or that sort of thing. Unfortunately, nature did not design him for the sheik part, having made him small, dry, and a little bald on top." In a letter to his son, Harrison expresses concern that his young wife finds his quiet and dull life boring and that a vacation to Paris will do her good. His son, then, hears a solicitous husband; but in Paris, as we learn in a letter to Munting from Lathom, Mr. Harrison inconsiderately stalked out of a cabaret, embarrassing his wife and Lathom. Agatha Milsom complains several times of Mr. Harrison's boorish and inconsiderate behavior. She nicknames him the Bear; his wife refers to him as the Gorgon in several letters to Lathom.

Munting says that Lathom accuses Harrison of brutality, a judgment he thinks is too harsh. Munting finally concludes to his fiancée, Elizabeth Drake, with whom he shares an honest and candid relationship unlike the Harrisons', that their quarrels prove "love makes no difference. Harrison would cheerfully die for his wife—but I can't imagine anything more offensive than dying for a person after you've been rude to them."

He does die for her, but not cheerfully. Gradually the documents reveal that Margaret and Lathom are having an affair. Just before we read Munting's account of finding Mr. Harrison's body, we read several letters from Mrs. Harrison who signs herself "Lolo." She complains that she cannot be an inspiration for profit and loss statements or electrical accounts. The letters addressed to "Petra" show that she has become Laura to Lathom, inspiring him to paint—and to murder—as Petrarch was inspired to write sonnets.

Eventually the murderer of George Harrison is convicted and executed after a recognizable sequence of related events, but about whom do we unqualifiably intone "guilty" for starting the sequence in the first place? Perhaps Margaret is guilty for inciting Lathom to murder. Can her personality or her letters to Lathom be considered as evidence of complicity? She never explicitly tells him to murder her husband. Perhaps Munting is guilty because he merely observes events without intervening. Maybe George Harrison's death is justified because his misguided notions of the husband's role impede the life of his wife.

The novel forces us away from simplistic mechanistic explanations of human personality at the same time it forces us to question the placing of responsibility. Lord Peter comes to recognize in *Unnatural Death* and in *The Nine Tailors* that we are all guilty. *The Documents in the Case* implies a similar possibility and warns of who, besides a court of law, judges us. In a key discussion toward the end of the novel, Munting, a group of scientists, and a curate discuss causal relationships. The physicist, Hoskyns, asserts that the universe cannot have originated by chance; the curate agrees, saying he calls the unifying principle "God." Sayers implicity cautions us to remember that we can be sure of death and of the higher judgment that follows. Unremittingly, the Harrison documents guide us through a tangled but passable garden of clues and deposit us in a clearing right in front of the body of George Harrison.

When we close the covers of any memorable novel, we usually recall one scene that epitomizes the work and calls forth sensations that remind us of what it means to be human. In *The Documents in the Case* that scene is George Harrison's bed, "broken and tilted grotesquely sideways," signs of violent dying in a lonely cabin. Munting mentions the bed once, twice, and then adds, "There was no peace in that twisted body and face. How long had the agony of delirium and convulsion lasted? It must be a damnable thing to die in so much pain, absolutely alone." Paul Harrison also comments on the broken bed "with its terrible witness to my poor father's death-agony. . . ."

After the sequence of events, after our evaluations of Mrs. Harrison and Mr. Harrison, we stop, finally, before that broken bed. In Sayers's works, dying is seldom more impressive than in *The Documents in the Case*. It is a novel of the progressive, not the past tense. As we reread it, the act of dying casts its long shadow over all else.

In most detective novels, says Sayers, "the victim is shown rather as a subject for the dissecting-table than as a husband and father." Although *Whose Body?* —which literally puts Sir Reuben on the dissecting table—and *Unnatural Death* leave us with victims that are more than impersonal mannikins, *Documents* goes further. It gives flesh and voice to the father-and-husband victim. Experimenting with lifelike characters in *Documents* seems to have made possible the creation of Harriet Vane in Sayers's next novel, *Strong Poison*. And with the creation of Harriet, Sayers felt it necessary to return her attention to her detective.

At the end of the twenties, Lord Peter Wimsey resembled the puppet Pinnochio more than a human being. Sayers confessed that when she began *Strong Poison*, she intended to marry Lord Peter off and get rid of him. Artistic integrity, a power stronger than love in fiction, prevented her accomplishing her aim. To have accepted Peter Wimsey's proposal anywhere in the novel was against the nature of Harriet Vane, although to rush into his arms would be acceptable in the tradition of popular romantic literature. In 1928

Sayers said, "Publishers and editors still labour under the delusion that all stories must have a nice young man and woman who have to be united in the last chapter." Such a union would not be consistent with the character of Harriet.

There was only one answer. "If the story was to go on Peter had got to become a complete human being. . . ." What began, however, as a transformation of character led to the fullest expression in prose fiction of Sayers's social values, as she put these two intelligent, lively characters together to work out their relationship intellectually, physically, and emotionally.

When she wrote *Strong Poison,* Sayers may have had in mind *Trent's Last Case,* a novel in which the detective falls in love and retires from detective work. She admired E. C. Bentley's achievement in that 1913 novel. She told readers that they may recognize its charm and brilliance and yet "have no idea how startlingly original it seemed when it first appeared. It shook the little world of the mystery novel like a revolution, and nothing was ever quite the same again. Every detective writer of today owes something, consciously or unconsciously, to its liberating and inspiring influence." Bentley brought a real human being into his novel to replace the infallible Holmes and the infallible and abstract Dupin.

Like Sayers later, Bentley was discontent with the overly mechanical detective story. He admired Holmes but did not admire his exaggerated unreality. When he began to write his novel, therefore, Bentley intended to depart from the Holmes model. The result was a novel that showed writers that they could break the pattern of the infallible, austere detective and still construct a unified plot. Sayers's discussion of *Trent's Last Case* praises its unity of plot and tone. Without violating its unity, she said, Bentley approached the detective novel as a novelist, not as a short-story writer of puzzles.

Although some people look to Sayers's friend Eric Whelpton as the model for Lord Peter, a more reasonable direction is toward Trent. His parodies of quotations ("the dun deer's hide on fleeter foot has never tied" and "drain not to its dregs the urn of bitter prophecy") resemble Wimsey's speech. As Trent's foolishness amuses Inspector Murch, Wimsey's amuses—and often annoys—Charles Parker. Not to push these comparisons too far, we need be aware only that when Sayers began to write, she looked to literature as well as to life for her models.

Before Lord Peter departed from her fiction, Sayers carefully operated on him to transform him from a puppet into a believable, three-dimensional character complete with genealogy and progeny. In 1937, she ruefully described her success: "I discover with alarm that his children are coming tumbling into the world before I have time to chronicle these events, and I am distracted and confused by the friendly letters of readers, giving him and Harriet the best advice upon child-welfare."

Before they could marry, however, Peter had to become as believable as Harriet. In *The Documents of the Case,* published the same year as *Strong Poison,* novelists John Munting and Elizabeth Drake anticipate the relationship that developed between Harriet Vane and Peter Wimsey. The honesty, friendship, respect, and affection of Munting and "Bungie"—qualities missing in the Harrison marriage—is the ideal toward which Harriet Vane reaches. As Harriet works through the dilemma of being able to marry and still remain true to herself and continue her work as a detective novelist, Sayers concentrates on the transformation of Lord Peter.

Harriet's values are literally on trial at the beginning of *Strong Poison.* The reader-juror listens to the judge's dry, parrotlike presentation of the Crown's accusation that Harriet Vane poisoned her ex-lover, Philip Boyes. She listens hopelessly and fearlessly to his summation of their living together for almost a year. Boyes had refused to marry her, saying that he did not believe in marriage. On February 1929, they quarreled. Harriet moved out. Her reason, the judge repeats, was that Boyes asked her to marry him after persuading her, against her better judgment, to live with him unmarried. By recanting and asking her to marry him, he renounced his previously argued principles and thus made a fool of her. The judge states that no other motive for murder has been presented.

Besides a motive, such as it is, Harriet Vane also had the means. As a detective novelist, she claims that she bought several poisons for research. Three times she and Philip Boyes met and each time he suffered from gastric attacks. On June 20, 1929, he and his cousin, the solicitor Norman Urquhart, dined together. Then Mr. Boyes left the house to visit Miss Vane. They drank coffee together. He was hardly able to return to Mr. Urquhart's. Three days later he died.

Harriet Vane had a motive, the means, and the opportunity. To Chief-Inspector Charles Parker, whose investigation had incarcerated her, Harriet Vane is guilty and the evidence establishes it. Lord Peter, who just happens to be at the trial where he sees Harriet for the first time, tells his friend that there is one flaw; she is innocent and he determines to prove it.

Miss Climpson, who happens to be on the jury, also defends Harriet. Aided by a male artist who understands the life and liberal values in the artistic community of Bloomsbury, and by an independent woman who owns a sweet shop, Miss Climpson prevents this trial from reaching a verdict. Another trial is set for one month later. In that month—December 1929 to the beginning of January 1930—passes the action of the rest of the novel.

Lord Peter's interest in the case results from more than a desire to prove his intuition right. In Chapter IV, he tells Harriet that he was stunned the first time he saw her and that he told his mother that here was the one and only woman for him. We begin to suspect as much in Chapter I, from his gloom in the courtroom and his curtly ignoring Freddy Arbuthnot's invitation to lunch, and going instead to confer with the defense lawyer, Sir Impey Biggs.

When he meets Harriet for the first time in Chapter IV, her steady gaze unsteadies him, her smile unnerves him, her candid answers about her relationship with Philip Boyes surprise him. He asks her to marry him, to which she responds with irony and polite humor.

From Chapter V on, we set off on the traditional chase to answer Who? and How? The murderer emerges about halfway through the book, leaving the answer to How? between Harriet Vane and execution. Since we never for a minute doubt that she will be saved, we just jounce along for the ride, which seems a bit airy after *The Documents in the Case.*

Miss Climpson goes to slapstick extremes to obtain evidence. She must secure the will of old Mrs. Wrayburn. Learning that the old, sick woman's nurse believes in spiritualism, a current fad, Miss Climpson holds a séance that interrupts the narrative with some comic moments. Her ingenuity supplies the motive for Boyes's murder. Another member of Miss Climpson's organization, Miss Murchison, learns to pick locks from Blindfold Bill Rumm, now a Salvation Army preacher. She discovers a forged will, which in turn sends Miss Climpson to seek the original.

Except for what *Strong Poison* ultimately produced, the continuation of the Vane-Wimsey relationship, the novel adds little to Sayers's canon. It does, however, reinforce one of her main social concerns, the situation of women. In Chapter V, the narrative discusses Miss Climpson's organization. Most of her employees are elderly; all are women. Their work not only gives them a purpose, but also protects others from the greed of men who prey on women.

Lord Peter's money supports the Climpson establishment. As we learned in Chapter III of *Unnatural Death*, not only is such a network useful to his detective work, it also proves that unmarried women, including the elderly, *want* to work. Only society keeps them from it and thus wastes a national resource. Lord Peter may get the credit for saving Harriet, but the women make it possible.

Besides his statements about society's mistreatment of women, Lord Peter's affection for and confidences with his mother and his sister and his friendship with Marjorie Phelps establish him as a character who flexes his heart, not his biceps. Philip Boyes, unlike Lord Peter, did not want a woman's friendship, but only her devotion.

In order for Harriet to marry Peter, however, she needs to be assured of his generosity of spirit, so rare in relationships between women and men. That he and she can be friends is suggested in her laughing and telling him that someone will probably marry him just to hear him "talk piffle." But he will need to do more than talk piffle to fulfill Sayers's goal to continue their story by transforming Peter into a complete human being.

4

FROM PUZZLE AND MANNERS TO MYSTERY
Five Red Herrings, Have His Carcase
Murder Must Advertise
The Nine Tailors

In a novel of manners, social customs, taboos, traditions, mores, religious and ethical beliefs impinge upon the characters and influence their actions and thoughts. Sayers claimed that she made her first serious attempt to combine manners with mystery in *Murder Must Advertise* (1933). We can recall that she had made experimental efforts before then. On the periphery of the murder to be solved in *the Unpleasantness at the Bellona Club,* for example, we find members of the post-war British society bowing to their dead traditions. *The Documents in the Case* suggests that an age of lethargic, indiscriminating beliefs creates a vacuum to be filled by such lifeless slogans as Respectability and Inspiration. The novel pulls us to its deadly center to impress upon us a society whose center is dead.

In *Murder Must Advertise,* Sayers declared, "the criticism of life was not relegated to incidental observations and character sketches, but was actually part of the plot, as it ought to be." In that novel we hear a solemn tone. Its actions lead us to recall the cabin scene in *The Documents in the Case* more readily than the jollity of Miss Climpson's séance in *Strong Poison.*

The year after *Murder Must Advertise* was published, Sayers wrote, in her introduction to the third series of *Great Short Stories of Detection, Mystery and Horror,* that detective and horror fiction had changed as the authors' sense of evil had changed. Earlier fiction included jolly sinners; "even their ghosts brought a kind of zest with them. But some of the new ones seem to come from a narrower and deeper and more intimate inferno; because we have realized only too well that the kingdom of hell is within us." *The Documents in the Case* took a jump forward in its recognition of the private inferno of an entire age. *The Five Red Herrings* (1931), which followed *Strong Poi-*

son, takes a step backward. Its successor, *Have His Carcase* (1932), looks forward to the social concerns of the Vane-Wimsey novels of the mid-1930s.

Five Red Herrings purports to be no more than the traditional puzzle novel. In her dedication to Joe Dignam, the landlord of her vacation cottage, Sayers proclaims that here is *his* novel, complete with real trains and correct landmarks. The novel is set in the landscape that surrounds the village Kirkcudbright in Galloway on the coast of Scotland and seems to have been written expressly for the entertainment of the inhabitants of that area, where Sayers and her husband vacationed each September.

She mimics dialects and prose styles to entertain her readers. Bunter, for example, enthusiastically paraphrases a servant girl's story about a "hollow groan" and "apparition" in the style of Horace Walpole's *The Castle of Otranto* (Chapter XV). And there is a humorous scene toward the end of the novel in which Wimsey and the police force re-enact the crime, assigning a role, including the corpse, for all the participants. Waiting to be transferred by automobile, the "corpse" becomes impatient and shouts from the garage. He is finally told, "corpse, you may sit up."

The comic exaggerations and the lack of psychological depth in the characters distance the reader from any human interests. No one sympathizes with the victim. All six suspects are so likable that we do not anticipate that any of them will hang. Lord Peter responds with detached politeness to the elaborate deductions of the police as though he were "an Eton boy applauding a good stroke by a Harrow captain."

The puzzle is so exaggerated that one suspects Sayers of having said, Okay, you want a pure puzzle; I'll give you a pure puzzle. Interviewing one of the suspects, Wimsey describes a novel that he may write, a novel that resembles the one Sayers wrote: "twenty chapters stinking with red herrings. . . ."

Murder Ink: The Mystery Reader's Companion explains the origin and meaning of the term "red herring." To throw hounds off the scent of the fox, antihunt people dragged smoked herrings through the woods. The fox would escape under cover of the strong odor of fish. It was not unlike Sayers, who relished play, to have created a book-length chase after fish odors. By the end of the book, we can imagine her asking the question that Gowan, one of the suspects, asks, "Did it work?"

In Chapter II, Campbell, a belligerent, unpopular painter, is found dead at the bottom of a cliff, a painting drying on an easel above. Although Campbell's death seems to be accidental, Lord Peter—who has become a temporary resident in Galloway—detects the right scent. Examining the area where Campbell was painting, he announces that he cannot find "IT," and thus knows that the death was no accident. Although Wimsey outlines five criteria for finding the murderer, IT remains the significant clue (and is not one of his criteria). Meanwhile, the police and the reader dash off after the five red herrings, a chase that lasts for more than twenty chapters. When the American edition, *Suspicious Characters*, was issued (by Brewer, Warren, and Putnam in September 1931), it included a blank page after Chapter II. The reader was invited to fill in the significant clue from which the murderer could be deduced. The puzzle depends on the reader's endurance, often aided by moments of humor and by chapter endings that wave the fox's tail to keep the chase alive. In his column "Behind the Blurbs" in *Outlook*, Walter R. Brooks in 1931 complained that one "might just as well have been reading higher mathematics" and that Sayers had let her readers down.

Becoming entangled in the lists and lists of train schedules may be as painful for many readers as the Chief Constable's fall into a tangle of bicycles. In leading us on by the question "Who did it?" Sayers almost masochistically trebles what she describes as the "Trials and Sorrows of a Mystery Writer." Rather petulantly, she explains in that essay that detective writers "are expected to know such a lot; not merely enormous subjects like medicine and law and finance and police organization, and engineering . . . but also tiresome little things like the time a railway porter might be expected to go to his tea. . . ."

Those tiresome little things, however, leave us finally with the impression of the work of a policeman. In the tradition of Edgar Allan Poe, Wimsey, like Dupin, does little of the plodding, tedious detail work. Like Dupin, he more often combines deductive reasoning with what Charles S. Pierce, the late nineteenth-century American philosopher, called abductive reasoning—a preference for one inference over another. We often think of these preferences as flashes of insight; Pierce included them in the reasoning process. In Poe's stories, the Prefect methodically adheres to deduction or induction. He painstakingly searches for missing objects that are right before his eyes or clues to a murder by resorting to tried and retried methods. By limiting his research to an inflexible thesis, the Prefect's failure is consistent. Poe satirizes so rigid a loyalty to methods and praises the more creative approach of Dupin. Sayers also demonstrates the superiority of Wimsey's cognitive agility that scans principles and patterns rather than fixing on details. The difference in her prefect—Sergeant Dalziel, in this case—is in her attitude to the worker. Unlike Poe's Prefect, Sergeant Dalziel, for all his methodical work, emerges from *Five Red Herrings* not as a buffoon, but as a dedicated, conscientious worker who continues his job even though he prefers to quit.

The puzzle continues until the very end of this long novel, when Wimsey solves it with the clue he found at the beginning.

When *Have His Carcase* was published the year after *Five Red Herrings*, readers found that they were in for more of the same. As one could expect, the reviews were similar to those of *Five Red Herrings*. In "A Book a Day," Bruce Catton informed potential buyers from California to Pennsylvania that in *Have His Carcase* "chances are ten to one you'll quit the book long before you reach the end. And, I might add, if you do you're smart. In fact, if you're really smart you won't even start it." If we never started it, however, we would miss more than just the solution to a puzzle.

The very similarities in the puzzles' structures inform us of the differences in the novels' effects. Because of the presence of Harriet Vane, *Have His Carcase* moves human-interest factors closer to the foreground. Because Harriet asks questions about human relationships, including her own relationship with Peter Wimsey, the murder and the environment in *Have His Carcase* are integrally related to the manners of the society in a way that they are not in *Five Red Herrings*.

Against a background of false and seductive values, Harriet Vane begins her search for equilibrium, a search that ends with *Gaudy Night* and *Busman's Honeymoon*. *Have His Carcase* sets the stage with a paragraph about how a woman recovers from a broken heart by work, exercise, and money. She does not fall into a man's arms in her search for stability.

We meet Harriet on June 18, 1931, on a walking tour along the coast from Lesston Hoe to Wilvercombe, a landscape created for the novel, in contrast to its predecessor which was created for the landscape. After her affair with Philip Boyes and her recently acquired wealth from the sales of her detective novels, Harriet Vane seeks spiritual renewal in the artfully arranged disorder of Lawrence Sterne's *Tristram Shandy* and a walk along the beach. She begins her walk early in the morning. By noon, she has a murder on her hands. She discovers a young man on a large rock, his throat so severely cut that his head nearly comes off as she examines it. She takes pictures of the corpse and some of its personal belongings.

The title of the novel plays on *habeas corpus* ("you have the body"), a phrase that designates a variety of writs about bringing a party to court or before a judge. In common usage, the phrase refers to the writ that protects against illegal confinement. In *Have His Carcase,* the body of the victim gets away. By the time Harriet Vane reaches the police, only her photos give evidence of the corpse, because the tides carry it to sea. It takes thirty-four chapters, each submitting evidence from a different source, to solve the murder of the man on the rock. Until then, of course, no one can be confined by the court.

Taking care of her own business before she begins to follow clues, Harriet dictates the story of the body to the London newspaper, the *Morning Star.* Strategically, she mentions her next book because the publicity will be good for sales. Lord Peter hears about the incident from his friend the reporter, Salcombe Hardy. He arrives in Wilvercombe to assist, asks Harriet to marry him, accepts her refusal with equanimity, and for the rest of the novel works with her to solve the murder.

In Chapter XIII, Harriet sarcastically begins to accuse Wimsey of galloping to her rescue so that she now has to feel grateful. She accuses him of a parade of chivalry, says that it is disgusting that a man thinks that by remaining superior a woman will tumble into his arms, and ends by saying that she recognizes that she is being ungrateful. He did save her life. At that point, Wimsey's silent endurance breaks: "Grateful! Good God! Am I never to get away from the bleat of that filthy adjective! I don't want gratitude. I don't even want love—I could make you give me that—of a sort. I want common honesty." There is no awkwardness in that speech. As in some of the dialogues between George Fentiman and his wife in *Bellona Club,* the sound of a human voice expresses one of the author's deepest concerns.

The values of work and common honesty have already appeared in Sayers's earlier novels. The relationship between John Munting and his fiancée, later to become his wife, Elizabeth Drake, forecasts the common honesty that Peter Wimsey finds with Harriet Vane. The friendship that began in *Strong Poison* continues in *Have His Carcase* and becomes an intellectual partnership. Sayers structured the novel not only to solve a mystery, but also to suggest the beginnings of Harriet's resolution to marry Peter. By working together they establish a foundation for their relationship. The chapters alternate between Lord Peter's and Harriet's investigations. His: "The Evidence of the First Barber"; hers: "The Evidence of the Gigolos"; his: "The Evidence of the Second Barber." Then together they explore the site of the murder in "The Evidence of the Flat Iron."

They discover that the victim was a young gigolo, Paul Alexis Goldschmidt, who worked in the largest hotel in town, the Resplendent, as a

professional dancing partner in its spacious lounge. A naturalized British
subject, he was rumored to have escaped from Russia during the 1917 Revolution.

Harriet and Peter learn that Paul Alexis thought he was a descendent of
the Romanov family, the family of the Tsars. The solution to the mystery
reveals that he shared a physical disability with the fated Romanov family, a
condition that no doubt intensified his belief in his royal heritage. To get
Paul Alexis to the Flat-Iron rock, the murderer sent him a cryptogram (the
Playfair code that John Rhode shared with Sayers). Wimsey and Vane decipher it by discovering its key word, *monarch.*

The murderer appealed to Alexis's susceptibility to romantic possibilities, which may have been encouraged by his physical disability and even
more, we can guess, by his taste in literature and film. Alexis's former
girlfriend, Leila Garland, tells Harriet that he liked thrillers about gangs. He
sought books and films in which the hero always wins. The strength of
Alexis's appetite for popular fiction, which fed his daydreams, not the weakness of his body, is the cause of his early death.

In the Resplendent microcosm, such ungenerative tastes dominate the
lives of its inhabitants. Leila Garland reads cheap romances such as *The Girl
Who Gave Her All.* The films pander to such preferences, as exemplified
when Bunter, trailing one of the suspects, is lead into a film of "Love and
Passion which shimmered and squeaked its mechanical way from the first
misunderstanding to the last lingering kiss." The philosophic gigolo, Mon-
sieur Antoine, evaluates the women who came to the lounge to find ephem-
eral excitement and love, which they think is happiness. He classifies them
as silly and says they ought to be happy they have healthy bodies. Instead
they come to him with their sorrows. In this, they resemble Margaret Harrison of *The Documents in The Case.*

When Harriet first enters the hotel in Chapter III, she watches the
dancers in the lounge. Dressed in costumes of the 1870s, the women mask
their faces in coyness and the strength and freedom of their bodies in expensive dresses that make their waists seem slim and fragile. Harriet wonders
whether men are "really stupid enough to believe that the good old days of
submissive womanhood could be brought back by milliners' fashions." The
women behind the masks hide their vital natures and independence.

In contrast, Harriet Vane does not. She has her work. She does not want
to be dependent upon a man. She wants to avoid the trap of false values that
Mrs. Weldon and the other inhabitants of the Resplendent world cling to. At
the same time, she does not want to live without physical and emotional love.

Harriet glances at an old woman who waits alone for her dancing partner, Alexis, who never comes. This is Harriet's first glimpse of Mrs. Weldon, whose exaggerated make-up disgusts Harriet, for it mocks rather than hides the old woman's age. Harriet later sees her more closely and more sympathetically when she talks with Mrs. Weldon about Alexis's death. Then the fear and grief that have ravaged the older woman's face so move Harriet that she averts hers. Mrs. Weldon's expressions of love for Paul Alexis nauseate and horrify Harriet by their artificiality. Her phrases sound as though they have been lifted from a trite magazine but, like the face under the cosmetics, Mrs. Weldon's emotion is genuine. It touches Harriet, who ponders whether, in her search for love, a woman's remaining alone always leads to as extreme a loss of dignity as Mrs. Weldon illustrates.

Because of Harriet's point of view, *Have His Carcase* includes with its murder mystery a consideration of the manners of the time. Like *The Documents in the Case* and *The Unpleasantness at the Bellona Club*, relationships between the sexes are woven into the plot of the novel. As the plot reveals the deadly consequence of a man's romantic dreams, we see in the character of Mrs. Weldon the consequence of a woman's living the popular daydream about tumbling into a man's arms.

Sayers suggests that perpetuating social fantasies about women's and men's actual selves is fatal. Women who mask their strength and freedom and seek book notions of romance find instead fear and grief. Men who believe in the daydreams of the romantic films and novels endanger themselves. The common honesty that Peter and Harriet seek offers a refreshing contrast. As Peter angrily states at the end of the novel, he despises the artifice of the watering place at Wilvercombe. Such false resplendence can offer little nourishment for the soul.

In the next novel, *Murder Must Advertise*, Sayers continues to dramatize the consequences of artifice that murders the spirit as brutally as the rider from the sea murdered Paul Alexis.

Murder Must Advertise tells a story about people who are either bored, rootless, and wealthy, or who are trapped in dull work, both of whom seek a life of material enrichment. The plot juxtaposes cocaine and advertising. The sling shot that murders Victor Dean and begins the action fires into the midst of British society.

When Dean, a copywriter at Pym's Publicity, falls down a dangerous iron staircase, the coroner's inquest ends with the verdict of accidental death. Pamela Dean, the sister of the deceased, sends Mr. Pym the fragment of a letter that she found in her brother's desk. The letter warns that something odd was going on in the conservative advertising agency. Mr. Pym hires Mr. Death Bredon to investigate (he does not know at first that he has actually hired Lord Peter Wimsey). Peter replaces Victor Dean as a copywriter, and he and the reader deduce early on that Dean was dead before he fell.

In this novel, How did he die? is answered soon; Who did it? next; and Why? last. By Chapter V, we know (1) that Dean was murdered; (2) that the weapon was ironically Dean's good-luck charm, an onyx scarab; (3) that because people constantly move around in an advertising agency, alibi will have little to do with this case; and (4) that an important clue will be the wild and wealthy crowd with whom Dean associated. Our curiosity about how Dean was murdered disappears and is replaced by our interest in Lord Peter's investigation to find out who and why. His search for the answers to those questions takes us to the center of the novel's social concerns.

As though she were describing a police lineup, Sayers places the murderer before us through the eyes of Pamela Dean as she watches the employees of Pym's Publicity:

> A brisk, neat young man, with an immaculate head of wavy brown hair, a minute dark moustache and very white teeth (Mr. Smayle, had she known it, group-manager for Dairyfields, Ltd); a large, bald man with a reddish, clean-shaven face and a masonic emblem (Mr. Harris of the Outdoor Publicity); a man of thirty-five, with rather sulky good looks and restless light eyes (Mr. Tallboy, brooding on the iniquities of Messrs. Toule & Jallop); a thin, prim, elderly man (Mr. Daniels); a plump little man with a good-natured grin and fair hair.

The reader can return to that passage at the end of the novel to ask whether or not the murderer distinguishes himself in any diabolical or obvious way.

In the second series of stories of detection and horror in 1931, Sayers notes in her introduction, "Murderers are on the whole less wicked than they were and victims less innocent—there is more light and shade about them both." As victim, Dean elicits little sympathy from either writer, reader, or characters. Similar to Campbell in *Five Red Herrings*, the best thing he ever did was to fall to his death. He remains more shadow than light. He did not play fair; he stole people's ideas and did not credit them for their help. Dean's actions were unethical but hardly motive for murder, as Wimsey discovers.

The victim remains in the shadow. The murderer steps to the foreground where we find that he has been motivated by a private hell. The murderer in this novel resembles the victim of the previous novel. Both are prey to false promises. The cryptogram that Alexis receives promises him fulfillment of his dreams of royalty. A materialistic society creates a dream of happiness for Dean's murderer.

As the novel unfolds, in case the reader does not begin to perceive the similarity between advertisers and the explicit villains, the dope pushers, Sayers has Parker say, "As far as I can make out, all advertisers are dope-merchants," a remark with which Peter agrees.

Yet even Peter, who understands the narcotic effect of advertising, is affected by it. In Chapter XVI, he talks in ad-copy prose when he asks Parker, "Are you tired at the end of the day? Do you suffer from torpor and lethargy after meals? Try Sparkletone." More seriously, he almost forgets why he is working at Pym's. As Mr. Bredon, Wimsey becomes so engrossed in his Whifflet Campaign that when Parker recalls him to his investigative duties, Wimsey curses.

In the line of duty, Wimsey distinguishes himself as Harlequin in order to find out more about the wealthy Dian de Momerie crowd with whom Victor Dean associated. The narrator tells us that Wimsey thus lives in two illusionary worlds—that of the world of advertising "rocking over a void of bankruptcy—a Cloud Cuckoo-land, peopled by pitiful ghosts"—and that of Harlequin. When he leaves one illusion, Wimsey becomes another, the "Harlequin of a dope-addict's dream; an advertising figure more crude and fanciful than any that postured in the columns of the Morning Star. . . ." The advertisements in the Morning Star affect the onlookers like Lord Peter's Harlequin affects the drugged Dian de Momerie. Like Harlequin, they promise an exotic life, "the Typist capturing the affections of Prince Charming by a liberal use of Muggins's Magnolia Face Cream."

At the end of the novel, the murderer, whose spirit has been killed long before his actual death by the dope mob, tells Lord Peter why he got involved with the drug ring and then murdered Dean to protect himself. In trying to find the good life—marriage, house, furniture—he found instead a trap; our verdict about this murderer: he is neither devil nor "Freke." He tells Peter, "You've got to keep going, and it breaks your heart and takes all the stuffing out of you." But these are not dolls, although the advertising images that the believers try to emulate are pitiful ghosts. As Mr. Bredon, Lord Peter learns that advertising is a drug not for the wealthy, but for "the comparatively poor . . . aching for luxury beyond their reach and for a leisure for ever denied them," a will-o'-the-wisp created by those who know how to arrange dreams in language.

In what could be a scene out of a thriller, Sayers demonstrates the power of language to move and to mislead us. In Chapter XV, two men tussle perilously close to the tracks of an approaching train. They topple and fall beneath the train. Then we read that the onlookers stand back while the porter and a helper bring something out from "between the train and platform. An arm came up, and then a head—then the battered body of the third man. . . . They laid him down on the platform bruised and bloody." For a moment, we grimly visualize the separate pieces of a chopped body. But the man opens his eyes and speaks. The syntax temporarily disguises the actual event.

In "Creative Mind," Sayers compared words to an electrical force and said that people ought not go about messing with them unthinkingly. Those who do know how to handle them have the advantage of those who do not. We are as vulnerable to the powers of words as "were the citizens of Rotterdam against assault from the air," she said in this 1940s essay.

In an earlier essay, "The Psychology of Advertising," she discussed the aim of advertisers to sell products by strategic use of words. "Like any other strategist, he assaults the weak places. Fear-gate, Sloth-gate, Greed-gate and Snob-gate are the four cardinal points at which the city of Mansoul can most effectively be besieged." The essay speaks directly to readers about the danger of false prophets. *Murder Must Advertise* works by indirection and drama to lead readers from the puzzle plot to reflection upon causes of spiritual crises in their society.

In *Have His Carcase* and *Murder Must Advertise*, the puzzles move us through the novels asking What happens next? Who did it? and Why? As we ask questions, we also perceive motifs that dramatize the false resplendence of contemporary manners—the association of cocaine and advertising in the latter novel, the fatality of daydreams in the former. As though she prophesied that the citizens of her country would soon be called upon to face a crisis, Sayers in the 1930s dramatized the acute and present danger of trusting daydreams and the glitter of materialism.

Because it is ever present, the Pied Piper's spell of advertising and mindless popular entertainment may seem as harmless as the murder weapon in *Murder Must Advertise*. Like the purloined letter in Poe's story, the scarab lay undetected for what it was. By advertising, murder almost succeeded. Only Wimsey was perceptive enough to really see the object. In this world of things-that-are-more-than-what-they-seem, Sayers suggests, one must be as observant as a detective. One must watch for the significance in the everyday and the familiar, which may camouflage an instrument of death, as in *Murder Must Advertise*.

Published the year after *Murder Must Advertise*, *The Nine Tailors* (1934) leads us by its puzzle to the revelation of God's world that co-exists with this world and transcends it.

Combining the disguises and aliases of *Unnatural Death* and *Have His Carcase*, the panorama of *Five Red Herrings*, and the hints of the supernatural from *Murder Must Advertise* and some of the Peter Wimsey short stories, *The Nine Tailors* remains a common favorite among Sayers's detective novels. And, yet, as we shall see in the next chapter, she was not completely satisfied. She was content, however, that she had successfully combined a sense of otherworldliness with the detective novel.*

Throughout *The Nine Tailors* the effects of the Fall are present: sin, change, death. In *The Documents in the Case*, Mr. Perry asserts, "We suffer for one another, as, indeed, we must, being all members one of another." *The Nine Tailors* dramatizes how that membership binds humanity to one another in culpability, responsibility, and—foremost—in joy.

Christian celebration sets the tone for the beginning of the novel. Change ringing in Fenchurch St. Paul in East Anglia establishes the context for the puzzle and is the novel's central metaphor for its action. When Lord Peter's car plunges down the side of a dyke in a snowstorm on New Year's Eve, he and Bunter walk toward the sound of a church clock. When they arrive at Fenchurch St. Paul, they meet the kindly rector, Mr. Venables, who invites them to be guests of his wife and himself.

Without knowing the full significance of his actions that New Year's Eve, Lord Peter joins Mr. Venables in his celebration of ringing out the old and ringing in the new years. Change ringing requires several ringers to pull the ropes of the eight big bells of the church. The ringers follow a pattern of precise alternations, or changes, of the bells. That New Year's Eve, one of the ringers, William Thoday, becomes ill; Lord Peter steps in as a substitute.

The next day, the bells again toll, this time for the death of one of the villagers, Lady Thorpe. As Mrs. Venables laments Lady Thorpe's death, she mentions the troubles that Sir Henry and Lady Thorpe have had. Always curious, Lord Peter wants to hear the rest of the story. He finds out that on the Thorpes' wedding day, one of the guests, Mrs. Wilbraham, had her emerald necklace stolen. Sir Henry's father vowed to repay her. He died, but Sir Henry fulfilled his father's pledge, losing most of his strength and fortune to do so.

---

*See John G. Cawelti's discussion of *The Nine Tailors* in *Adventure, Mystery, and Romance* (Chicago: The University of Chicago Press, 1976), pp. 120–25.

Several months after Lord Peter's stay in Fenchurch St. Paul, Sir Henry himself dies. The puzzle plot begins on Easter Sunday, the day of Sir Henry's burial beside his wife. To the gravediggers' surprise, they unearth a man's body in Lady Thorpe's grave. Whose body? Why is its face mutilated and its hands severed at the wrists? How did the man die? Who buried him in Lady Thorpe's grave? Mr. Venables writes Lord Peter to help find an answer to these questions and in the meantime, he directs that for a second time that day the nine tailors toll.

The title of the novel refers to the code that tolls a person's death. The tailor bell tolls six times for women, nine for men. When Mr. Godfrey shows the now orphaned Hilary Thorpe the bell tower, she reads the inscription of the bell Tailor Paul: NINE + TAYLORS + MAKE + A + MANNE + IN + CHRIST + IS + DETH + ATT + END + IN + ADAM + YAT + BEGANNE +.

Like *Documents in the Case, The Nine Tailors* gradually moves us closer and closer to the moment of dying. Late in the novel, Lord Peter talks with a primary suspect, Nobby Cranton, who saw the body's face before it was slashed, a face like he never wants to see again. He exclaims, "Just as though he'd been struck dead and mad all at one go, if you see what I mean." Another witness also describes the dead man's face: "He'd died on his feet, and whatever it was, he'd seen it coming to him. . . . And his face! My God, sir. I've never seen anything like it. His eyes staring open and a look in them as if he'd looked down into hell."

God's presence, in the physical shape of the church and its bells, hovers over the actions of men in this novel. Several times onlookers respond to the bells as though they were strangely alive. When Lord Peter agrees with Nobby Cranton about their mysteriousness, the orthodox Christian, Charles Parker derides him. Wimsey tells Parker to wait until he gets caught in a dark belfry. "Bells are like cats and mirrors—they're always queer, and it doesn't do to think too much about them." Mr. Godfrey explains to Hilary Thorpe that when Cromwell sent his men to break up the church's icons, the bell Batty Thomas swung down on a soldier, killing him. The bell saved the church because the other soldiers fled.

The presence of the bells in *The Nine Tailors* increases in significance as we begin to see that change ringing is the main thread in Sayers's design of the novel, including the solution to the puzzle of the corpse. By her consistent use of the terminology of change ringing to entitle the chapters, Sayers explicitly establishes change ringing as the context for the novel's actions. The individual chapter headings denote the investigative actions in each chapter and, more significantly, taken altogether, the chapter headings suggest an analogy between the activity of investigation and the cooperative activity of change ringing. The necessary cooperation in both activities gets us back to the theme of humanity's bonding ties of membership.

In the chapter entitled "Plain Hunting," the title denotes the importance of the detective action. The "Plain Hunt" pattern of change ringing is basic to most of the other patterns. Similarly, in that chapter, Hilary's sending Lord Peter a cryptogram and Superintendent Blundell's locating Nobby Cranton are the bases for further investigations that reveal the relationship between the puzzling corpse and Mrs. Wilbraham's missing emeralds.

The language of change ringing in the title "Lord Peter Dodges with Mr. Blundell and Passes Him" denotes the method of the detectives and also implies an analogy between their work and change ringing. In that chapter, the two detectives seek the answer to who put the unidentified corpse in Mrs. Thorpe's grave. The chapter alternates between Mr. Blundell's and Lord Peter's investigations, like the "dodge," or alternations of one pair of bells.

Like change ringing, the investigations in *The Nine Tailors* depends upon the collective work of many individuals. To solve the puzzle, Sayers brings in skilled amateurs, such as Lord Peter, and professionals from the most experienced officers to the ordinary policeman. Together they gather information that reveals the complex connections among Will and Mary Thoday; Nobby Cranton's partner, Deacon; and Mrs. Wilbraham's emeralds. With the aid of French Commissaire Rozier of Chateau-Thierry, Chief Inspector Charles Parker of London, and Superintendent Blundell of Leamholt (which is near Fenchurch St. Paul), Peter and Bunter search for answers to the puzzle.

Gradually, change ringing thickens into a metaphor of more than a community's activity. It becomes a metaphor of the human condition. Hezekiah offers the following advice to Lord Peter, "Make righteousness your course bell, my lord, an' keep a-follerin' on her an' she'll see you through your changes till Death calls you to stand."

Changes dominate the landscape of *The Nine Tailors*. As Lord Peter and Bunter journey to Leamholt to follow a hunch about the corpse's identity, the narrator describes the landscape. Now flat and inland, the area used to be a great port. The signs of change remain "with her maritime tradition written unerringly upon her grey stones and timber warehouses, and the long lines of her half-deserted quays." When he is having lunch at a local inn, Wimsey converses with the waiter about the drainage project (which later floods the area and is the subject of the apocalyptic final chapters). The project, a large drainage ditch to carry the tide from the river, will improve the land, returning it to its condition in the days of Cromwell, the waiter says.

In "The Waters Are Called Home," the most exciting section of the novel, the old gates burst and the waters flood the land surrounding Fenchurch St. Paul. Peter climbs the tower. He looks out over a sea where there had been solid ground. He sees abandoned villages, the place where the Wale River should be, and water covering the site where two men drowned in the fury of the flood.

Before he can escape to safety away from the clanging rage of the bells, Lord Peter discovers the answer to the most horrific change of all—the mutilated corpse's face. At the same time, he recognizes his and the other change ringers' complicity in its horror. "In the midst of life . . . we are in death," acknowledges Mr. Lavender early in the novel.

Sayers's book draws us forward to ascend that tower with Wimsey and experience its revelation. Amid the changes and dangers, the church remains stolid and unchanging. God's truth remains and His judgment prevails. Mrs. Venables remarks darkly that "there are always wheels within wheels." Almost like the opening of the seven seals in the Revelation of St. John the Divine, Sayers's novel unfolds its design, its wheels within wheels. We begin in joyful celebration, during which one man suffers dreadfully—although we later believe deservedly, for he was a thief and a murderer. As the novel draws us through its motifs of change ringing and changes from the past to the present. Hezekiah's advice lingers like the echo from a tolling bell.

The novel *The Nine Tailors* ends with a retelling of the story of the flood in Genesis, a story that reminds us of God's promise and unchanging grace. Humorously, Peter Wimsey re-enacts that promise when he swims in the flooded village street and returns with a laurel branch.

Mingled with the solid textures of this world is the power of another. "The snow was still falling fast; even the footprints made less than an hour earlier by the ringers were almost obliterated. They straggled down the drive and crossed the road. Ahead of them, the great bulk of the church loomed dark and gigantic." Like their disappearing footprints, people and landmarks change and pass, but looming over all is the mysterious shape of God's design. The changes of mankind work out God's plan, His wheels within wheels. Mr. Venables says that he never thought he would thank God for the war, for example, but it taught the people the alarm code of the bells that saved them from the flood.

Similar to Sayers's earlier novels, *The Nine Tailors* speaks to an age of disbelief groping for meaning in transitory and false values. In *The Documents in the Case* the false prophet is respectability; in *Have His Carcase* and *Murder Must Advertise*, romance and resplendence. Guiding us by its puzzle, *The Nine Tailors* opens before us a higher reality the path of which—if we observe it clearly—is here on earth.

In *The Nine Tailors* Sayers emulates Wilkie Collins as she evokes from the reader a sense of God's mystery. For her His presence leaves us with a sense of terror (the dead man's face and the apocalyptic flood) and glory (Fenchurch St. Paul and the bells). And believing in both and serving as our model is the compassionate, amiable servant of the Lord, Mr. Venables.

5
PRECARIOUS BALANCE
Gaudy Night
Busman's Honeymoon

The Nine Tailors remains for many readers Sayers's best detective novel. Its activities and its landscape expand significantly with the unfolding mystery to take in heaven and earth. *Gaudy Night* is as layered as *The Nine Tailors* is panoramic. Character development integrates ideas and manners with the puzzle in Sayers's penultimate novel.

The puzzle mystery resolves Harriet Vane's dilemma, which began in *Strong Poison* and continued in *Have His Carcase*. As *Gaudy Night* answers the question "Who is disrupting the peace of Shrewsbury College?" it also begins to answer the questions that Harriet has asked about her own peace: How can this intelligent working woman, without compromising herself, marry the wealthy aristocrat who has saved her life? How can she be true to herself without living for or at the expense of another? What happens to people that prevents their living together harmoniously? By posing these questions, Sayers's *Gaudy Night* and its successor, *Busman's Honeymoon*, consider the difficulty of maintaining the delicate balance of human relationships.

Recalling her context, the years between two world wars, we recognize the source of Sayers's concerns. In *The Long Week End* (1941), eye-witnesses Robert Graves and Alan Hodge comment upon the mid-thirties: "The international situation was already disturbingly unsettled. It was clear that collective security was only a phrase, and that power politics had returned in full force."

In *Busman's Honeymoon*, the celebration at the beginning dramatizes the joy of a different, a creative, power. To arrive at the full creative powers of her own work and in her characters' lives, Sayers gradually clarified her

71

vision and her skills as an artist. Her joy at having found her voice is evident in the following statement about *Gaudy Night:* "By choosing a plot that should exhibit intellectual integrity as the one great permanent value in an emotionally unstable world I should be saying the thing that, in a confused way, I had been wanting to say all my life."

Her enthusiasm is not always shared by her critics. In *Mortal Consequences*, Julian Symons brushes *Gaudy Night* aside with a statement that would very probably rankle Sayers. He calls the novel "essentially a 'woman's novel,'" whatever that means. If it means the novel features women, he is correct. Sayers concentrates on one community of women scholars at Shrewsbury College, Oxford, where trust and peace ordinarily reign. The disruption of the enclosed garden of Academe brings Harriet back to that garden where she solves her personal dilemma.

Some detective-novel fans may begin to ask, after reading several chapters of *Gaudy Night,* Well? Where is the murder? And where, for form's sake, is the detective? Lord Peter Wimsey does not even show up until more than halfway through the book. What kind of detective story *is* this, anyway? Such responses would resemble those in the review by Mary McCarthy in *The Nation,* when the novel was published. It has, she says, no murder, no action, no problem, no mystery. It does not, in other words, conform to the expected formula. We know by now, however, from Sayers's earlier works and from her remarks about the detective novel that she intended to change the formula. She retained the structure of the detective novel to present a puzzle that asks "Who did it?" but placed it in the context of a novel of manners, which asks "Why do individuals behave as they do? What social pressures influence them?" More closely related to *The Documents in the Case* than to *Five Red Herrings* or even to *Strong Poison, Gaudy Night* ponders the difficulty of maintaining harmonious human relationships.

The action of the novel takes place from June 1934 to May 1935. The setting is Shrewsbury College, modeled after Sayers's own college, Somerville. The action begins when Harriet Vane returns to Shrewsbury for a college reunion, or Gaudy. While she is there for the weekend, she finds signs of unpleasantness in the form of perverse notes that have been dropped on the ground and in the sleeve of her academic gown. One says, YOU DIRTY MURDERESS. AREN'T YOU ASHAMED TO SHOW YOUR FACE? Considering her past, Harriet thinks the note is intended only for her.

When she receives a letter a few months later from Letitia Martin, the Dean of the College, Harriet learns that someone is directing a campaign against the entire faculty and student body. Miss Martin requests that Harriet help them solve the mystery of the combination Poltergeist/Poison Pen. The administration wants no help from the police. The reputation of women's colleges may be in jeopardy if people begin to think that, driven by sexual repression, some unmarried, cloistered don lectures high ideals that disguise a perverted mind. That stereotypical view muddies even Harriet's usual clarity. The Poltergeist continues to rage; for over a year, she hangs Shrewsbury women in effigy, destroys their books, and leaves suggestive and threatening notes.

Harriet works alone for thirteen chapters to try to solve the mystery. She communicates with Lord Peter, but he has been sent out of the country. In Chapter XIV, her communications finally reach him. From then on, Harriet and Peter work together to stop the threats, but not before the Poison Pen becomes murderous. After the disrupter's capture in the final pages of the novel, Oxford returns to the peace of the enclosed garden; Harriet solves her dilemma, which signals Peter's final and complete transformation from caricature to human; Peter and Harriet exchange formal and tender vows of commitment.

On its surface, *Gaudy Night* resembles a romantic fairy tale, complete with a good magician, evil spirit, and foreboding prophecies. For example, the first chapter creates a sinister atmosphere for the events to come. As Harriet looks through an old trunk, its contents provide a material review of her past, a review in which she has been mentally engaged since she received the invitation to the Shrewsbury Gaudy. In the trunk she finds old shoes, old manuscripts, even an old tie that belonged to Philip Boyes, and her M. A. gown and cap. The past and future are implicitly connected when she brushes some material loose from her academic cap. From the material, "a tortoise-shell butterfly, disturbed from its hibernation beneath the flap of the trunk-lid, fluttered out into the brightness of the window, where it was caught and held by a cobweb." To be caught has been Harriet's fate. Is it to be repeated?

Since the trial concerning the death of Philip Boyes, Lord Peter has continued to ask Harriet to marry him. The beginning scene of *Gaudy Night* melodramatically suggests that she is in danger of awakening from her hibernation in work to enter a deadlier one. To avoid the trap of sexual relationships, will Harriet overdo her dependence on work? At Shrewsbury, she picks up a page of the English Tutor's magnum opus on prosody. Miss Lydgate warns her, "Don't prick your finger on that bit of manuscript that's pinned on." Like Sleeping Beauty, who pricks her finger on a spindle and falls into a deep sleep, will Harriet fall asleep to life until she is awakened by the kiss of a handsome prince who penetrates the tangles and briers that cover the palace gate?

One night as Harriet works on her LeFanu study and has just begun to revise a passage about the supernatural, the lights mysteriously go out all over the campus (Chapter IX). Just as mysteriously, Lord Peter appears on a bright Sunday morning after a May thunderstorm. The technique resembles those of the short stories in which he appears like the good spirit of a fairy tale.

The atmospheric touches and implicit comparisons to fairy tales are not gratuitous in *Gaudy Night*. It *is* a fairy tale for the modern age. Those persons who find the answers to the questions that Harriet asks can maintain a stage of perilous, reflective balance, as Peter and Harriet ultimately do. Such people live as happily ever after as twentieth-century people can.

Since *Strong Poison*, Harriet Vane has tried to avoid the trap of traditional socio-sexual relationships without putting her sexuality permanently to sleep. In *Gaudy Night*, her dilemma is to decide whether her writing and scholarship, a life devoted to independent work, will be more satisfactory than a life with Lord Peter. Even better, if there could be a synthesis, she would not have to choose. She wonders if she somehow can integrate the two, the intellect and the emotions. The solutions to her dilemma and to the mystery of the vindictive notes crisscross.

We learn late in the novel that six years before the action in *Gaudy Night*, the husband of the sender of the notes had suppressed some information so that his professional thesis would pass an examining committee. Miss de Vine, who was on the committee, discovered the indiscretion, and exposed him. He lost his professorship and his M.A. The poison pen has been dipped in venom against Miss de Vine and women scholars in general. But the letter writer is not sexually repressed in the way that Harriet thinks at first. She repressed herself in the service of her husband and is now seeking revenge. Her narrow perception of the roles of the sexes forces her to blame Miss de Vine and other women at Shrewsbury for not doing their jobs, which to this woman means tending to a husband and children. In the context of *Gaudy Night* that view is a perversion of the emotions over the intellect. Miss de Vine, however, also learns that her own action was imbalanced. She emphasized the intellect over the emotions. She learns that one can combine both.

To reach this solution and the solution of the mystery, the novel gradually draws us away from the chaos and disruption caused by the Poison Pen's anger to the Senior Common Room of Shrewsbury and a civilized, rational conversation. In that same chapter, Chapter XVII, Harriet Vane begins to discern the solution to her personal dilemma.

The detective puzzle begins in the first three chapters of the novel when Harriet finds the two sadistic and accusatory notes. Her own puzzle begins there also. She realizes that she must make a decision about Peter, who has continued to pursue her for five years. Although he has been good natured about her hesitation, she knows that now she must decide once and for all what her relationship with him is to be. During the weekend of the Gaudy she considers specific examples of sexual relationships.

As she prepares to attend the Shrewsbury Gaudy, Harriet thinks about Mary Stokes, her friend in college. Since graduation, Mary had married and disappeared except to attend every reunion. When Harriet sees her, "Mary Stokes (now Mary Atwood) seemed cut off from them, by sickness, by marriage, by—it was no use to blink the truth—by a kind of mental stagnation." The stagnation, Harriet concludes, has nothing to do with either marriage or sickness. Certainly her former friend is no model for Harriet.

Catherine Freemantle's situation is no closer to the problem that Harriet faces if she marries. Brilliant, lively, an outstanding scholar of her year, Catherine Freemantle married a farmer, whose way of life has erased her devotion to scholarship. Now as Mrs. Bendick, she tells Harriet that her former classmates live in a dream; they know nothing about real life. Harriet says that she respects Catherine's principle of loyalty, but reflects, "I'm sure one should do one's own job, however trivial, and not persuade one's self into doing somebody else's, however noble."

Another classmate, Phoebe Tucker, had married and was able to remain true to her ideals and potential. A history student, she married an archaeologist. Their partnership has produced children and pamphlets as they travel around the world to lecture and to dig up pottery, bones, and stones. When Peter Wimsey offered himself to Harriet in *Strong Poison*, he, too, avoided the conventional *Kinder, Kirche, Küche* approach to marriage. He admitted that he would like to have someone interesting to talk to.

By the end of the first three chapters of *Gaudy Night*, Harriet has three models for marriage, two of which she has no taste for. She rejects the retreat into marriage of Mary Stokes and the call of misguided duty of Catherine Freemantle. But to be married like Phoebe Tucker may be impossible, especially because Lord Peter's social class and aristocratic heritage as lord of the manor makes his talk of equality between them suspect to Harriet.

She then begins to assess the situation of the unmarried scholars. She enjoys her renewed vitality in the scholarship she pursues at Oxford and the peace that the closed garden of the university provides. She writes one-half of a sonnet to express her feeling of being at home and safe from life's storms. But she cannot finish the poem.

As she looks at the lives of the scholars, Harriet finds that Miss Lydgate's and the Dean's seem to be fulfilled. But what about Miss Hillyard, the History Tutor? Miss Hillyard's bitterness about the inequality of society's views of the sexes enters almost all her conversations. Her rejection of the traditional maternal role takes the form of a strong bias against Mrs. Goodwin, the Secretary, who must be absent several times to care for her sick child. Harriet thinks to herself how "difficult it was not to be embittered by personal experience. . . . There had been a look in the History Tutor's eyes that she did not wish to discover in her own." Her behavior suggests to Harriet that Miss Hillyard responds out of a personal loss that goes beyond an antipathy to sexual politics, a loss that Harriet may be repeating if she rejects Peter Wimsey.

Like Eiluned Price in *Strong Poison*, Miss Hillyard's attitude suggests the direction that Harriet's experience with Philip Boyes could take her. In Chapter VIII of *Strong Poison*, Lord Peter tries to conform to the code of gentlemanly behavior by carrying a kettle of water for Eiluned. She takes the kettle and quips acidly, "No thanks. . . . I'm quite capable of carrying six pints of water." Marjorie Phelps explains that "Eiluned disapproves of conventional courtesies between the sexes." Conventional courtesies imply the old imperialistic protection, which demands devotion in return. Like strong poison, those implications must be avoided. Harriet must decide whether avoiding the ancient forms means rejecting heterosexual relationships.

A union between Harriet Vane and Peter Wimsey must be a marriage of minds and values as well as a marriage of the flesh. The first three chapters of *Gaudy Night* implicitly ask the question that Harriet and Peter will mutually answer: "Could there ever be any alliance between the intellect and the flesh?" Their answer and the answer of the novel are affirmative.

Chapter XVII brings us to the heart of the matter, for in addition to its presenting the central clue to the mystery, this chapter reinforces Peter's and Harriet's central value of intellectual integrity. It also dramatizes the possibility of a balance between one's intellectual ideals and one's emotional concern for others.

The question of a balance between the emotions and the intellect appears in a novel that Lord Peter, Harriet, and the dons discuss in Chapter XVII, C. P. Snow's *The Search*. Snow's novel also contains the clue to Poison Pen's motive, especially if we remember that in Chapter XII we were told that pages 327–40 of Snow's novel had been mutilated. In the conversation of Chapter XVII, Dean Martin summarizes the story found on those pages: The main character, Arthur Miles, discovers that his friend Charles Sheriff violated scientific ethics when he suppressed information so that his research would appear to be successful. Later we understand that the fictional situation is similar to that of the husband of Annie Wilson, the letter writer. The resolutions are different.

In Snow's novel, Miles knows of the suppressed information because he had abandoned the same research years before when the results did not tally. Consequently, he lost an important post and the girl he loved when she married Sheriff. Miles drafts a letter to the periodical that published Sheriff's findings with the intention of exposing him. Then he pauses to consider whether there is something stronger than the conscience of science and his love of science. If he does not send the letter, would that mean he has given up science irrevocably? If he does send the letter, what would it do to his friend? Sheriff would lose prestige and the respect of his wife. Miles does not send the letter—in contrast to Miss de Vine who had to make a similar decision. In her anger, we conclude, Annie ripped out the pages that showed that one *can* place another human's life above an intellectual standard.

The discussion in Chapter XVII integrates the thematic issue of the balance between intellectual standards and emotions with the detective mystery. From the discussion, Peter infers the significance and motive of the nasty notes. The women learn the importance of tempering intellectual standards with human emotions. They agree that Miss de Vine's real-life counterpart to Snow's character of Sheriff was unscrupulous. Not even his having lied about his research to benefit his family could redeem him.

How could a woman live with such a man? Miss Chilperic timidly offers that a woman would feel as if she were living on immoral earnings. And Lord Peter makes a key statement that could be used as the coda for Dorothy L. Sayers's books about Harriet Vane and Peter Wimsey: "But if it ever occurs to people to value the honour of the mind equally with the honour of the body, we shall get a social revolution of a quite unparalled sort." Just about then, as if to disrupt such revolutionary talk, Annie asks for Harriet's coffee cup.

From the discussion, from her actions, and from the consequences, Miss de Vine learns a lesson. She does not blame herself for remaining true to her intellectual standards, but she does recognize that she could have been more like Miss Lydgate, who in the same circumstances would have been more compassionate, who would have made sure that she found out what happened to the man and his family (Chapter XXII). One need not compromise the intellect to acknowledge the emotional needs of another human, admits Miss de Vine, but she also warns Harriet that the "Marriage of two independent and equally irritable intelligences seems to me reckless to the point of insanity. You can hurt one another so dreadfully." Before Harriet's dilemma can be fully resolved she must decide whether she and Peter can live as equals and, if so, whether Miss de Vine's conclusion would apply to them.

On the day of Peter Wimsey's unannounced appearance at Oxford, the two of them go to Harriet's room to talk. They both wear academic robes and caps, which they had worn to the church service. His robe represents his achievement in History in which he took a First; hers, English in which she, too, took a First. In her room, their gowns lay side by side. When Peter leaves in a rush to keep an appointment, he takes her gown by mistake. She decides that it makes no difference because they are about the same height and stature.

They work together to catch the Shrewsbury terror. They match wits in quotations in Latin and French. Their intellects are evidentally compatible. They also hold the same values about work. Besides their shared information about the Shrewsbury mystery (his work), they talk about her problem with a character in her novel (her work). Resembling Sayers's character of Lord Peter, Harriet Vane's character Wilfred needs to become human. As they discuss this technical problem, Harriet recognizes that Peter takes her seriously and also that he is brutally honest. She perceptively admits to herself, just as she is about to let resentment disrupt the talk, that he responds to her work and not to her as a female. "The protective male? He was being about as protective as a can-opener."

His standard of honesty matches her own. In *Strong Poison*, Ryland Vaughn complains that Harriet Vane would not advise her novelist-lover, Philip Boyes. Vaughn erroneously attributes her refusal to comment on Boyes's writing to women's behavior, to a hatred of men and their work. Actually, her integrity motivates her. She would never lie about her reaction. Philip wanted devotion; therefore, she responded with silence rather than pander to his desire to be worshipped.

Intellectual compatibility and ethical agreement have evolved from *Strong Poison* and *Have His Carcase* to *Gaudy Night*. In the latter, Harriet also decides that body and mind do not have to be separated; there can be an alliance between the intellect and the flesh. Before they enter the Senior Common Room in Chapter XVII, Harriet slips her hand under Wimsey's arm and feels reassured by his humanness. As she puts her hand on his arm, she thinks that they are of the same world. It is a world of the same ideals; it is also a concrete world of the flesh and facts.

For her characters to get to this point, however, Dorothy Sayers had concentrated for several years on the character of Lord Peter.

After *Strong Poison* she was disappointed but not discouraged by the caricaturelike Wimsey. She reviewed his character and came to the conclusion that the chances were favorable to produce a believable character with a believable past, present, and future, a character with an inner as well as a public life.

When she reevaluated her detective's assets in 1930, she determined that he had a past—his service and wound in World War I, his love for the woman who spurned him (mentioned in *Clouds of Witness*). He had a present—with his mother, sister, brother, and valet Bunter, who had served in the war with him. He had friends—Charles, Freddy, and acquaintances at his many clubs. He also had hobbies and a distinctive personality. Here were items that Sayers could expand upon.

He even had the rudiments of a psychology—his distaste for the consequences of his detecting, and his nightmares. Her novels had therefore given Sayers something to work with. Although in the earlier works Wimsey tap-dances into a detective problem, in *Whose Body?* his nerves attack him, partly a consequence of having been in the war and, we can infer, partly brought on by his recognition of his part in another's death. In *Unnatural Death*, he seeks spiritual advice about his responsibility in the death of innocent people. As he begins to suspect the murderer in *Strong Poison* and recognizes the inevitable result of his suspicion, he tells himself, "I'm beginning to dislike this job of getting people hanged." In *Busman's Honeymoon* (1937), dislike increases to gloom.

Conscientiously transforming her detective into a believable human, Sayers deepened his inner life, developed his family, and increased his age. When we first meet Lord Peter in the short stories, he is in his early thirties. In *Strong Poison*, he tells Marjorie Phelps that he is going on forty (Chapter VIII). In Chapter II of *Gaudy Night*, Harriet tells Miss de Vine that he is forty-five (in Chapter VII, we find out that she will be thirty-two). When we last see him in "Talboys," Lord Peter is fifty-two. To be believable, he must act his age. Sayers sarcastically recalls one reader's lament that in *Gaudy Night* Peter had lost his elfin charm. She "replied that any man who retained elfin charm at the age of forty-five should be put in a lethal chamber."

That Lord Peter is the logical result of generations of Wimseys seems to be without question and shows how well Sayers succeeded in giving her

puppet human qualities. His biography was the result of careful prepara-
tion.* In *Strong Poison* Wimsey mentions the original Gerald de Wimsey and
tells Harriet that the family motto is "I hold by my Whimsy." In *Busman's
Honeymoon* Lord Peter shows Harriet the family portraits at Bredon Hall;
some of his relatives were associated with Queen Elizabeth. For the complete
genealogy, one need not search through Sayers's novels; C. W. Scott-Giles's
The Wimsey Family (1977) combines references from the novels and short
stories with personal correspondence from Sayers.

The first time an official biography appeared was in an anthology of
short stories edited by Kenneth Macgowan, *Sleuths: Twenty-Three Great Detectives of Fiction and Their Best Stories* (1931). Part of this biography appears in *Murder Must Advertise* (1933). When Miss Meteyard becomes suspicious of the mysterious Mr. Bredon, she turns to *Who's Who* to read:
"Wimsey, Peter Death Bredon (Lord), D.S.O., born 1890; second *s.* of Mor-
timer Gerald Bredon Wimsey, 15th Duke of Denver, and Honoria Lucasta,
d. of Francis Delegardie of Bellingham Manor, Bucks. *Educ.* Eton College
and Balliol."

As the pivotal novel in the transformation of Lord Peter, *Strong Poison*
(1930) not only signals the tip of an impressive genealogy, it also reaches
forward to give Wimsey a future and to deepen his character. Chapter XII
begins, "Wimsey was accustomed to say, when he was an old man and more
talkative even than usual, that the recollection of that Christmas [1929] at
Duke's Denver had haunted him every night regularly, for the following
twenty years." One reason was that during that Christmas holiday he had
begun to suspect the murderer of Philip Boyes and thus to dislike the results
of detecting. Besides beginning to dislike being the cause for a hanging, he
knows that his accuracy will save—or his inaccuracy doom—Harriet Vane.

Later, biography and psychology come together in *The Nine Tailors*
(1934), which begins on New Year's Eve 1929 in the Fen Country. From
Have His Carcase (1932) we learn that his family lives "in Norfolk—Duke's
Denver, on the borders of the Fen country." We can infer that all the while he
is home for Christmas 1929, Harriet Vane's case is on his mind. On his
return to London, he and Bunter have the accident at the beginning of *The
Nine Tailors* and have to spend the night at Fenchurch St. Paul. Again we
can now imagine that his thoughts were very likely on London and the Boyes
trial while he was change ringing that New Year's Eve.

---

*See Alzina Stone Dale's "Fossils in Cloud-Cuckoo Land," *The Sayers Review*, III (December
1978, pp. 1–13) and "The Whimsey Saga: A Chronology" by G. A. Lee and Alzina Stone Dale
in the same issue, pp. 14–20.

Arriving at this understanding of the effect of Christmas at Denver, then, we can see why Lord Peter accepts Hilary Thorpe's invitation to spend the following Christmas with her. The invitation gives him an excuse for not having to go to Denver, which "was most disagreeable to him." Lord Peter has never liked Gerald's wife, but putting the events of *Strong Poison* together with those of *The Nine Tailors* allows us to determine that Peter's dislike of Denver involves more than his dislike of his sister-in-law. It reminds him of the Philip Boyes murder. Our own game-playing, then, indicates how well Sayers succeeded in integrating—or causing us to integrate— the psychology and the biography of her detective.

In addition to having given Lord Peter a public record and a private life, Sayers also gave him flesh. In *Strong Poison* he tells Harriet that he makes love "rather nicely." In subsequent novels, Sayers worked on his sex appeal. In *Murder Must Advertise*, dressed as Harlequin, Wimsey enthralls Dian de Momerie by a perfectly executed dive from the top of a fountain. They next meet in the forest. Again Wimsey dresses as Harlequin; anything but unreal, however, he lifts her up "and she felt his hands hard as iron under her breast." A cliché perhaps, particularly in the age that produced *Lady Chatterley's Lover*, but we can recognize Sayers's attempt. To be human, especially a prospective groom, Wimsey must have sexuality.

And to be human, one is also vulnerable. *Have His Carcase* presents his sexuality and vulnerability from Harriet Vane's point of view. She observes his shoulders and calves as he runs down the sand in his swimming suit and concludes that they are passable. In the same scene, Sayers calls on a comic device from her short stories to deflate her detective to ungodlike proportions. He asks Harriet a question as his head stands "up sleek as a seal's out of the water."

Wimsey's sexuality and vulnerability reach their most concrete in *Gaudy Night*. Peter has returned from a journey of pre-war diplomacy; exhausted, he sleeps in a boat while Harriet watches. From her point of view, his flesh becomes tactile. In a slow, sensuous scrutiny, she notices details of his half-averted face. "The gleam of gold down on the cheekbone. The wide spring of the nostril. An almost imperceptible beading of sweat on the upper lip and a tiny muscle that twitched the sensitive corner of the mouth."

Death, of which sleep reminds us, is our ultimate vulnerability. Of Peter's mortality we see horrifying evidence in *The Nine Tailors*, when blood runs from his nose and ears as he tries to escape from the bell tower.

Even after *The Nine Tailors*, however, Sayers's detective still remained a problem to her. To be a hero not only of a detective novel, but also a novel of manners, he needed more than flesh, sexuality, and genealogy. When she assessed *The Nine Tailors,* Sayers was not satisfied. She saw that she had fulfilled one goal in her appeal to human sensations. In her puzzle she had integrated the sensations of this world with the suggestions of a transcendent world of deeper mystery. She had not, she declared, accomplished the synthesis of Peter Wimsey, detective, and Peter Wimsey, hero of a novel of manners. He remained "extraneous to the story and untouched by its spiritual conflicts. This was correct practice for a detective hero, but not for the hero of a novel of manners." To be both, he must not only resolve conflicts, he must be touched by them.

The conflict that touches him the deepest is Harriet Vane's. Her hesitancy to marry Lord Peter arises from mores that govern relationships between women and men. Those mores form the central social issues in *Gaudy Night* and also underlie its mystery. By resolving the social issue of a woman's and a man's mutual respect, Harriet resolves her personal dilemma. Entering the discussion about the relationship between a man and a woman and intelligence and emotion, thus ultimately solving the Shrewsbury mystery, Peter Wimsey is drawn into the center of a detective novel of manners.

The moment when Harriet slips her hand under Peter's arm represents the end of a long evolution of Sayers's art and the beginning of a new model for sexual relationships. Out of traditional forms, Sayers aimed to create a new form of detective novel that included serious attention to manners. Out of traditional social forms, she dramatized a new model of relationships between women and men. In a world of change, Sayers recognized that old forms can be clung to and atrophy; she also knew that they could be injected with new life.

In the same way that Peter completes the prescribed form of Harriet's sonnet in *Gaudy Night,* he will complete her life; and she, his. By remaining true to their values and respect for each other they can achieve a revolution within the traditional form of marriage. In the final scene of the novel, Harriet and Peter give fresh meaning to another old form. Instead of avoiding the old courtesies, they create a new context for them. As they pass through the shadows of the walls of New College and stand in the pale sunlight, Harriet tries to find the word that will speak her acceptance of Wimsey's proposal.

> It was he who found it for her. With a gesture of submission he bared his head and stood gravely, the square cap dangling in his hand.
> "Placetne, magistra?"
> "Placet."

The words are relics from an important political ritual from Roman and medieval times. They are now a pro-forma gesture of good will used to approve decisions of the administration at Oxford, the affirmative reply of the assembled Magistri to the question, "Does it please you?" Lord Peter asks, "Does it please you, Lady Master?" to which Harriet responds that it pleases her. She completely accepts him and by using these words as a dialogue of love, Peter and Harriet revivify an old language and old form.

But with life come dangers. Harriet understands that she and Peter can hurt each other dreadfully, for their energies make harmony only a temporary still point. In the scene where she feels that the two of them are of the same world and all others are different, Harriet also experiences a conflicting emotion. When she is with those of her sex, she suddenly sees Wimsey as "a dangerous alien and herself on the side of the women." She will experience similar emotions in *Busman's Honeymoon*, but they will not destroy the center of their union. To live often entails conflicting emotions that hurt deeply.

In *Gaudy Night*, when she discovers Peter's sestet that completes her sonnet, Harriet learns that Peter "did not want to forget, or to be quiet, or to be spared things, or to stay put. All he wanted was some kind of central stability, and he was apparently ready to take anything that came along, so long as it stimulated him to keep that precarious balance."

Sayers felt that in *Gaudy Night* she had reached her apogee. Lord Peter's transformation was complete; Harriet Vane could therefore marry him. Her decision to accept his proposal and the solution to the puzzle of the threatening notes at Shrewsbury College allowed Sayers to merge the novel of manners and the detective novel. Her aim, which manifested itself as early as *The Unpleasantness at the Bellona Club*, was to synthesize the human and the mechanical interests. Often, to balance them was difficult achievement enough. But as she learned to merge human and detective interests, Sayers also learned what she had to say about human relationships, about the power of love and mutual respect. In her next and last novel, *Busman's Honeymoon*, Harriet and Peter put what she had learned to a test.

In contrast with its sinister beginning, *Gaudy Night* ends with a lyrical description of the setting and creates a mood that the opening of *Busman's Honeymoon* reinforces. In *Gaudy Night*, the rain over, buildings shine clean and clear in the sun. As Peter walks away in the distance, Harriet has all of Oxford shimmering around her as she surveys the glittering landscape, but she sees only, "one slight figure that crossed the cobbled Square, walking lightly under the shadow of St. Mary's into the High. All the kingdoms of the world and the glory of them." This beatific vision precedes the final scene in which Peter and Harriet pledge their commitment to each other. It looks forward to a fulfillment of his code of joyful sex. There can be no worse sin, he has postulated, than for sex to be joyless, a sin that he and Harriet will not commit. But they will have moments of separateness and pain.

The joy of the final pages of *Gaudy Night* is continued in the symphonic first five chapters of *Busman's Honeymoon*, in which Mr. Puffet, Miss Twitterton, and Mr. Goodacre join Peter and Harriet in song. Their joy is rapturous—until it is disrupted by a murder. The disruption tests the perilous balance between joyful union and painful separateness.

In February 1935, Dorothy Sayers and a close friend from her days at Somerville College, Muriel St. Clare Byrne, began work on a play about Lord Peter. The play, *Busman's Honeymoon*, opened in December 1936 at the Comedy Theatre in London's West End, running in successful competition with T. S. Eliot's *Murder in the Cathedral*. The novel was begun after the play. Both were published in 1937.

Busman's Honeymoon, subtitled *A Love Story with Detective Interruptions*, begins late in the evening of the Wimseys' wedding day, October 8, 1935. Peter and Harriet travel to the Elizabethan village where Peter has purchased the cottage Talboys. When she was a child in the next village, Harriet's ambition had been to own the quaint farmhouse. In a mood of joyful homecoming, the Wimseys occupy their honeymoon house. By October 11, however, they have discovered a body, investigated a murder, and captured the criminal. Mr. Lavender's remark in *The Nine Tailors* could serve as an appropriate epigraph: "In the midst of life . . . we are in death"—including the Elizabethan sexual play on the word "death."

As Harriet and Peter joyfully consummate their marriage upstairs in the goosefeather bed, the body of the former owner, William Noakes, lies in the basement. Bunter discovers the body the next day during the happy community celebration. In Chapter VI, the novel begins to answer the conventional detective questions of How? and Who? Sayers's primary interest in *Busman's Honeymoon*, however, is not the mechanics of the puzzle, but its related side issues that illuminate the relationship between Harriet and Peter Wimsey.

Like other Sayers victims, Noakes seemed to have asked to be murdered. He was greedy. He was blackmailing the patrolman, Joe Sellon—young, married, father-to-be. Noakes also owed Frank Crutchley money, money that he needed to start his own garage. The question is why he was murdered? When he died, he had with him much of the money that Lord Peter had paid him for Talboys. Robbery, then, was not the motive.

Again Harriet and Peter work together to arrive at answers. Peter exclaims his pleasure at her matching his ratiocinations. She has no idea, he says, "how refreshing it is to talk to somebody who has a grasp of method." In turn, when he says that first one needs to show how the crime was committed and then "bring in motive to back up your proof," she repays his compliment. She seems to have married her "only intelligent reader."

Like a new Adam, Wimsey was created for Harriet Vane who was, said Sayers, human from the beginning. The success of this pair produces an ideal of married life. By the end of *Gaudy Night*, which culminates an evolution from *Strong Poison* through *Have His Carcase*, they are friends and intellectual partners. They honor each other, mind and body. The situation in *Busman's Honeymoon* gives their creator the traditional context of marriage in which to test their relationship.

In Chapter X, glum and moody, Lord Peter abstractedly builds a house of cards. Harriet tries to cheer him. The house of cards falls. She remains silent as he begins to build it again. The scene may seem to portend the failure of their life together, but it does not. She remains silent to let him find his own answer to his disappointment about the interrupted honeymoon. Finally he attributes his sullen humor to vanity, the lordship's desire to bend Providence, to have the perfect honeymoon. Humbly recognizing his vanity, he regains perspective. Had they been ten years younger, the narrator explains, the scene would have included tears, harsh words, and reconciliation by embrace. As it is, husband and wife rationally talk about their conflicting feelings. As Peter had respected her emotions for five years, so Harriet now respects his.

Even when they are together, then, they recognize the walls of separation, as in the scene above. Harriet again feels the gulf between them, just as she had felt in *Gaudy Night* when, as she and Peter descended the stairs to enter the Senior Common Room, she suddenly sensed him to be alien. In *Busman's Honeymoon*, their genders again separate them. Like the scene on the stairs in *Gaudy Night*, simultaneously with the joy of their partnership, Harriet experiences moments of painful separateness. The conflicting emotions occur because of the behavior of the murderer, Frank Crutchley. His villainy is not only his murder of Noakes, but his misuse of Agnes Twitterton, who loves him. In her sympathy for Agnes, Harriet suddenly experiences a separateness from Peter, an alienation from all men.

They have just arrived at Talboys from a community gathering at the vicar's. In loving joy they sing; they talk of love. As in the first chapter, coming home characterizes their metaphors for their relationship. Harriet reflects that all of her life she had been wandering until she found him. In his arms, she is satisfied. He responds, "I love you—I am at rest with you—I have come home." Meanwhile, Agnes Twitterton has been hiding upstairs. Embarrassed at having been crying over Frank Crutchley, she tries to avoid the Wimseys; but on hearing their words of love, she cries out in anguish. Harriet goes to her; Peter leaves the women alone. In the distance, they hear him below speaking harshly to Bunter about the port that Mrs. Ruddle ruined. As their voices recede, the women breathe "more freely. The dreadful menace of male violence lifted its shadow from the house."

Later, Harriet and Peter almost reach an impasse about Agnes Twitterton. Peter enumerates the reasons that she could have murdered her uncle. Her alibi for the night of the murder is suspicious; she has a motive. Harriet suddenly finds herself in the position of the C. P. Snow character. She wants to protect Agnes Twitterton. Peter allows Harriet her position, but he reminds her that one cannot choose to withhold evidence or proof. "Whoever suffers, we *must* have the truth. Nothing else matters a damn."

Incidents such as these, which arise from the puzzle plot, test the Wimsey marriage. They reaffirm Harriet's and Peter's values from *Gaudy Night*, love with honor, no matrimonial blackmail, no corruption of power. Integrity will maintain the delicate balance of living together. To be bound does not mean to possess.

For two decades of writing detective fiction, Dorothy L. Sayers had explored relationships of women and men. Harriet and Peter Wimsey represent the best in an ideal world where power is not asserted by force but by love. Knowing at the end of the 1930s war was looming ahead makes such idealism understandable. But, Sayers, matching the fiction with the facts and being concerned for the soul of her country, began to turn away from games of whodunit. We can hear Peter Wimsey's farewell by examining several scenes of *Busman's Honeymoon* and by comparing the novel with the play.

When Bunter discovers the body in the play and in the novel, Peter curses, not the exuberant "Damn!" that introduces *Whose Body?* but an expletive of discouragement: "Damn . . . And damn! Back to the old grind. *Rigor mortis* and who saw-him-last, blood-prints, finger-prints, foot-prints, information received and it-is-my-dooty-to-warn-you." In both the play and the novel, these lines seem to echo Dorothy Sayers's own weariness with the detective form.

In the play, as in the novel, when the police lead the murderer away, Peter turns to Harriet and says, "This part always gets me down." At the end of the play, they embrace, and the curtain falls. The novel goes further, as its medium allows. Peter engages Impey Biggs to defend the indefensible as his atonement for being responsible for bringing the murderer to justice. But on the night of the execution, Lord Peter leaves the house, a practice that Bunter has seen before. Peter returns at 4:00 A.M. to wait out the final hours with his wife. The novel ends not on the upbeat of the play but in despair, with Lord Peter's head huddled in Harriet's arms, which muffle the sound of the clock striking the hour of execution.

Like the last scene in *Busman's Honeymoon*, a scene near the end of Sayers's incomplete novel *Thrones, Dominations* leaves no doubt that Lord Peter is through. In that scene, he walks into Charles Parker's office, where they discuss the recent death of King George V (January 1936). Peter feels that with King George's death, he has lost a standard as well as his youth. He feels as though he has grown old in a moment, he tells Charles. And cryptically he remarks that King George stood for "something" that he shall miss. In *Documents in the Case* Lathom cynically comments that only the suburbs believe in anything, that the aristocracy "has lost the one belief that made it tolerable—its belief in itself." Perhaps it is the strength of King George's belief in himself that Lord Peter shall miss.

Certainly in *Busman's Honeymoon* and in the incomplete *Thrones, Dominations*, Lord Peter no longer believes in himself as the brash character who applied for the job of detective "complete with spats and . . . an airy don't-care-if-I-don't-get-it" manner. His time is up. In *Thrones, Dominations* Charles asks Peter to accompany him to Bloomsbury, where Charles must seek out political agitators. Peter refuses, saying that political agitators have no title to crime.

The times and the types of crime fiction have changed. Lord Peter no longer belongs. Charles has to stay to complete his job, but their work together is over. In the scene above, he watches Peter's slow departure and, then, feeling depressed, he picks up the list of agitators.

For over fifteen years, Sayers believed in the possibilities of detective fiction, not only for her times but also for her own developing expression. She created a fictional hero that fights for the right, for truth over falsity, and for human relationships based on love, honor, and compassion. Now that she herself had learned what she had been trying to say all her life, now that her detective had grown older (his age is 45 in *Busman's Honeymoon*) and world weary, Peter Wimsey could retire. Except for a few stories of *In the Teeth of*

Evidence (1939), "Talboys" (which was written in 1942 but not published until 1972), and some unfinished manuscripts, Sayers put away her detective fiction after 1937.

During the early years of World War II, her characters spoke for her in the "Wimsey Papers," published in *The Spectator*. They voiced her concerns for her society, but she no longer wrote their stories. By then, she had turned to religious drama and to translations, of which the most well known is Dante's *Divine Comedy*. The puzzle solving that both Peter Wimsey and his creator had taken up so blithely in the early 1920s had run its course.

VALUES AND AESTHETICS: A TOUCH OF THE ETERNAL IN SAYERS'S DETECTIVE FICTION

In the 1940s, Sayers compared her society's response to art with that of Plato and Aristotle, who, like her, lived during an era of crises. Her discussion of what people looked for in art resembles the characterization Mr. Perry offers in *The Documents in the Case,* when he says that as a result of the first war people believe in everything—spiritualism, the daily papers, anything, because it is easy.

Of the public response to art from the 1920s to the 1940s, Sayers comments:

> We too have audiences and critics and newspapers assessing every play and book and novel in terms of its "entertainment value," and a whole generation of young men and women who dream over novels and wallow in day-dreaming at the cinema, and who seemed to be in a fair way of doping themselves into complete irresponsibility over the conduct of life until war came, as it did to Greece, to jerk them back to reality.

Sayers continues her comparison by saying that the Greek civilization collapsed; her own had not—yet.

In January 26, 1940, in "Wimsey Papers—XI" of *The Spectator,* Lord Peter pleads with his wife to speak to the people, to tell them that they were waging a war that could be won on the battlefield and lost at home. He tells her to arouse them and "make them understand that their salvation is in themselves and in each separate man and woman among them. . . . [T]he important thing is each man's *personal responsibility.*" Sayers's detective fiction dramatizes her gradually developing acknowledgement of Lord Peter's imperative.

Sayers's readers not only follow a densely populated trail of clues; we also participate in the almost magical process of literature, the pull of an artistic design toward gradually increasing awareness of a truth about humanity beyond the event of the puzzle. By the end of *The Nine Tailors,* for example, we not only understand the title as an allusion to the death of an unidentified man, we also realize its significance. Taken as a whole, the novel heightens the injunction that we ask not for whom the bell tolls. Vividly we are reminded that it tolls for each of us. We recognize our experience in Sayers's and in John Donne's before her.

If the artist is faithful to her art, she presents a truth that "is new, startling, and perhaps shattering—and yet it comes to us with a sense of familiarity." It is new because the artist creates it and we witness the design in the making. It is familiar because we share her discovery, which becomes ours. The true artist, Sayers affirmed, cries, "Look! recognize your own experience in my own." First, though, Sayers had to learn what her own was.

Sayers's detective fiction gave her a way to discover her times and society. Her last works, for example, include actual places that she had known— the advertising agency, the Fen country, and Oxford. Sayers's detective writings share with her readers her gradual recognition of the values that she associated with these places: the mixture of economic necessity and psychological strategy that characterizes the advertising world, the close association of the natural and divine worlds in the Fen country of her childhood, the significance of intellectual standards and work that she had witnessed as a student at Oxford. What Sayers had blithely begun in order to earn money and to enjoy herself also revealed to her significant connections among the loss of integrity, traditional woman-man relationships, and war.

Her fiction does not dope the reader into irresponsibility over the conduct of life. Although the detective form always punishes the criminal, Sayers was not eager to reassure her audience that such a comfortable pattern of poetic justice characterizes human life. As *The Nine Tailors* dramatizes, we are all members of one another; we are all responsible.

Looking back from the perspective of a second world war, Sayers argued that to categorize war or crime as problems to be solved in the manner of a detective novel leads people astray. They begin to think of death as the evil, whereas they ought to pay attention to the chaos that war brings to the survivors. If they do not, they will direct all their resources "to evading war at all costs, rather than to dealing intelligently with the conditions of life which cause wars and are caused by wars." That evasion, she said, characterized her society between World Wars I and II. In her detective fiction of the twenties and thirties, as we have seen, conduct and the conditions of human life had always been central.

Later, after she had stopped writing detective stories and retired her characters from fiction, she brought them back during the first years of the second world war to speak for her in *The Spectator,* as Lord Peter does when he asks Harriet to use her talents to arouse the citizens. And in an excerpt from a supposed sermon on Armistice Sunday, Sayers spoke through the persona of the Reverend Theodore Venables, who concluded that "the whole interval between this war and the last had been indeed a period of armistice—not peace at all, but only an armed truce with evil."

Looking back over Sayers's detective fiction, we find that it dramatizes one source of the evil—faulty attitudes toward work. The right attitude manifests itself in creative joy and vitality, a touch of the eternal. For example, Peter Wimsey's work of detecting usually intoxicates him. The excitement he shares with Charles Parker as they follow the movements of the Person Unknown in *Clouds of Witness* and that he and Harriet share as they decode the cipher in *Have His Carcase* emanates as much from the love of creating order out of fragments of information as from his respect for the truth and work well done.

His intoxication resembles that of the change ringer. To the onlooker, the narrator of *The Nine Tailors* explains, the eight intense faces in the spellbound circle of ringers may seem to be absurd. However, their concentration signals the "solemn intoxication that comes of intricate ritual faultlessly performed." Lord Peter's capers and energetic conversation signify his intoxication. Like the change ringers who find pleasure in making music, Lord Peter finds pleasure in making sense. There is one major difference, of course. His work results in the life or the death of someone, the gravity of which, as we have seen, Lord Peter likes less and less. Nevertheless, he does his job with dedication.

"It's the work you're doing that really counts," Harriet Vane recalls the Dean saying in *Gaudy Night.* Miss Lydgate tells Harriet that one need not be a scholar, but one ought to do her best: "I think it's so nice that our students go out and do such varied and interesting things, provided they do them well."

Detectives, writers, scholars, change ringers have one value in common: their dedication to the quality of their work, a feature one finds often among artists. Mr. Crowder of "The Unsolved Puzzle of the Man with No

Face," for example, refuses to flatter his subject for money or position. He upholds the integrity of his expression by painting Mr. Plant's portrait honestly, no matter how unflattering it may be. Harriet refuses to compromise her art to please Philip Boyes in *Strong Poison*.

Without being an artist by profession, Lord Peter views his work artistically. In *The Nine Tailors*, he calls the case of the extra corpse "beautiful" and "charming." He regards the case in *Unnatural Death* "beautiful in its ease and simplicity." *The Unpleasantness at the Bellona Club* presents him with "a very pleasin' and pretty little problem." Wimsey's aesthetic approach to his work and the vitality of his joy in its performance establishes him as a special hero—the model worker.

We have already noted that Wimsey is both human and mythic. Golden arrows point the way to his aid; he appears as a voice out of the shadows or seems to materialize out of thin air after a thunderstorm. A passage in *Clouds of Witness* suggests his fairy-godfather character: "In the frightful silence which followed . . . the sound of a walking-stick being clattered into an umbrella stand was distinctly audible." Help is on its way.

Wimsey represents the spirit of good in the world. As guardian of decency, protector of the right uses of knowledge and beauty, he crusades against the violators of common dignity and worth. Sayers called the detective "the latest of the popular heroes, the true successor of Roland and Lancelot."

As mythic hero, Wimsey helps the needy; as human, he offers a model for people to help themselves. In 1940, as we have seen, Sayers spoke in Wimsey's voice to plead for personal responsibility; in 1942, she spoke in her own. She prophesied that what happened to civilization would depend upon attitudes about work. "It is, or it should be," she declared in *Creed or Chaos*, "the full expression of the worker's faculties, the thing in which he finds spiritual, mental, and bodily satisfaction, and the medium in which he offers himself to God."

If we approach our work in love, we can, like the Divine Creator, survey it and declare it good. We then participate in the divine pattern: "The characteristic common to God and man is apparently that: the desire and ability to make things." For Sayers, work is "a sacrament and manifestation of man's creative energy." These expository statements of her values appeared almost a decade after she had ceased to write detective stories. Their dramatic expression, however, lives in her portrayals of Wimsey and other likeable and energetic characters.

When Things Ain't Done,
They Won't Do 'Em

Admirable people in Sayers's fictional world follow a code of right behavior. Superintendent Kirk of *Busman's Honeymoon* expounds on Lord and Lady Wimsey's code that "when things ain't done, they won't do 'em—and that's the long and short of it." The same can be said for all of Sayers's good characters. They uphold codes of honor and integrity about their work.

To Peter's question in *Whose Body?* about whether or not he likes his job, Charles Parker answers that he does. He explains that he does it well enough to be proud of it and he likes its variety that "forces one to keep up to the mark and not get slack." As we can trust Charles to do his job well, we can trust him to keep his word. He assures Hector Puncheon, the young reporter of *Murder Must Advertise,* that for sharing information with the police, Puncheon will have all the details first if the police learn anything. "I can't say fairer than that," Charles tells Hector.

Montague Egg's mottoes about business articulate his belief in a job not only professionally but also ethically well done. Egg protests to the Inspector in "False Weight" in *In the Teeth of Evidence,* that the last thing a commercial traveller would do is to steal another's sample case. "There was freemasonry of the road."

From Mr. Egg to Mr. Parker, Sayers's likeable characters approach their work in love. Mr. Puffett's exuberance as he cleans the chimneys, Miss Climpson's jovial stamina as she seeks information, Lord Peter's verbosity as he follows clues, Harriet Vane's joy as she researches Sheridan LeFanu—all are manifestations of the worker's creative energy, that energy which originates in the eternal energy of God. Whether Sayers's workers are selling wine, writing books, or collecting data, they serve their work in joy. Similarly, her own work celebrates her creative energy. The complexities of the puzzles in *Five Red Herrings* and *Have His Carcase* and the intricacies of the design in *The Nine Tailors* and *Gaudy Night* resemble songs in multiple keys.

Sayers's best characters serve their work; they do not ask that it serve them. Parker, for instance, often illustrates the discomforts that one must endure to complete tasks. We watch the privileged Wimsey drive away in a taxi as Charles walks to the bus; Wimsey dines sumptuously in one of his clubs while Charles has an unappetizing meal in a café that smells of stale grease. Parker and others like him from the early to the late detective novels have work to do and they do it "and that's the long and short of it." After the high pitch of the final chapters of *The Nine Tailors*, the novel ends with the commonplace. Superintendent Blundell wishes Wimsey and the others a good morning and walks out of the door, presumably to pursue another laborious puzzle.

The villains or questionable characters misuse their work. They do not serve it. Mr. Garrick Drury of "Blood Sacrifice," in *In the Teeth of Evidence*, violates his theatrical art. As an actor, he wants only those vehicles that appeal to the public. As a producer, he takes advantage of the young playwright John Scales, who needs money. Drury turns Scales's honest play into a sentimental pleasure dome for the public. Scales complains; he thinks of the money he receives as "wages of sin"; nevertheless, he takes it.

In *Strong Poison*, Norman Urquhart abuses his position as family lawyer and trustee of an estate. Similarly, Dr. Penberthy of *The Unpleasantness at the Bellona Club* takes advantage of his authority as General Fentiman's physician. In *Unnatural Death*, Mary Whittaker uses her nursing skills to commit murder. Julian Freke diabolically uses his surgical skills to flaunt his crime.

By misusing their work, Sayers's criminals sin against God. They disrupt the divine pattern of creative energy, at least temporarily. Although evil cannot be abolished, it can be redeemed by creative power. To Sayers, creativity meant synthesis, making something new out of the materials that one has. One does not destroy in order to create, one assimilates the old with the new. Sayers's belief applied to her view of art as well as to her view of society. "The good that emerges from a conflict of values cannot arise from the total condemnation or destruction of one set of values, but only from the building of a new value, sustained like an arch, by the tension of the original two," she stated.

The marriage between Harriet Vane and Peter Wimsey concretely dramatizes a synthesis of values—Peter's aristocratic, male-dominated heritage with Harriet's contemporary, feminist views. Individually, they are dedicated to their work—Harriet to shaping words; Peter to shaping facts. Together, they provide models for the social revolution that, in *Gaudy Night*, Lord Peter foresees.

Harriet and Peter Like Each Other; They Share a Laboratory Together

Revolution for women and men will occur, Sayers predicted, when they recognize the value of work. Lord Peter and Harriet Vane are not just a romantic duo created to titillate the audience. Transformed for Harriet, Lord Peter is no longer a caricature but a human. These protagonists can thus be seen as a contemporary version of Adam and Eve, working not in sorrow but in joy. As they respect their own work and each other's, so they respect and honor each other.

J. R. R. Tolkien complained that although he found Lord Peter attractive at first, by the time he read *Gaudy Night* his loathing for Wimsey was "not surpassed by any other character in literature known to me, unless by his Harriet." In response to the Vane-Wimsey novels other readers sometimes may be tempted to repeat Tolkien's words. Certain passages overstate Harriet's "normality" to show that she is not like Mary Whittaker. To demonstrate that Harriet can be independent and "womanly" at the same time, Sayers's prose sometimes sounds as though it were lifted from the books that Leila Garland read. In *Have His Carcase*, as Harriet dances with Peter, she reflects that he ought to compliment her. When he does not, she becomes "convinced that she was dancing like a wax doll with sawdust legs."

Harriet sometimes sounds as though her head contains the sawdust. In Chapter XVI of *Have His Carcase*, Peter suspects that the murderer approached the death site on horseback. To confirm his suspicions, he interviews a farmer. Sayers as narrator makes a point of interrupting the farmer's comments with parenthetical attention to Harriet's confusion. "No, he never mowed the meadow on account of the (agricultural and botanical detail of which Harriet did not grasp the significance) . . . (interminable historical detail . . . in which Harriet becomes completely lost)." Such interruptions spare the writer, and mercifully, the reader from having to be bothered with tiresome details. One does wonder, however, why Sayers chose Harriet's bewilderment as her way out of technical difficulties.

One reason may be that Harriet's confusion is a literary device to keep the vocations of Lord Peter and Harriet Vane distinct. Her specialty is writing; his, detecting. In her detective novels, Harriet can discard information that may be troublesome. For example, in *Have His Carcase* she admits that her detective Robert Templeton is a sloppy dresser so that she can avoid having to keep up with the subtleties of men's fashions. By contrast, the detective cannot omit details. In "real life" Wimsey must use what he finds. He must pay attention to the data he collects to determine their relationships; Harriet can collect only that data for which she will construct relationships.

Besides suggesting their different jobs, the self-conscious treatment of Harriet Vane may also be attributed to a situation that Virginia Woolf described in *A Room of One's Own* (1929). She suggested the following hypo-

thetical passage: "Chloe liked Olivia. They shared a laboratory together."
Woolf then said how startling that passage was. There was no tradition for it
and, yet, certainly "women, like men, have other interests besides the per-
ennial interests of domesticity." Perhaps Sayers was also attempting something that popular literature had given her little language to do—to show a
friendship and respect developing between a woman and a man, a respect
and friendship that allow them to follow their own interests and still care for each
other.

In *Busman's Honeymoon,* Sayers overwrites the scene where Wimsey
begins to put the pieces of the puzzle together. His eyes pass over his wife as
though she were a stranger. They meet Bunter's eyes, Bunter, his companion
through a hundred cases. When he does finally see Harriet, he speaks to her
as though she were a servant (Chapter XX). We can detect the same self-
conscious writing in the descriptions of Harriet's bewilderment in *Have His
Carcase.* Very likely, Sayers attempted to say, "Harriet and Peter like each
other. They share a laboratory together although they make different things
there."

It served Sayers's art of manners as well as her values to give Harriet
and Peter separate vocations. To her there was no such thing as "woman's
work" and "man's work." There was only work. In her 1938 address, "Are
Women Human?" she stated that everyone "*must* have occupation, if he or
she is not to become a nuisance to the world."

A woman and a man find that after the war, the man cannot work. His
wife must. Still, he accuses her of being an upstart, of not knowing her place
(The Unpleasantness at the Bellona Club). A woman gives up her work for her
husband. He thinks that his wife ought to cleave unto him only. She desires a
separate life *(The Documents in the Case).* An independent woman, intelligent, artistic, has her work as a novelist. She is attracted to a man who is also
intelligent and who appreciates the arts. She has learned from one experience, however, that sexual attraction and intellectual equality do not guarantee a successful relationship between a man and a woman. To be content, she
must have a marriage with honor or forfeit marriage altogether, a loss that
could lead to bitterness.

These synopses indicate one of Sayers's pervasive topics—traditional
relationships between men and women and their attitudes about work. In her
fiction, these relationships express not only whatever actual conflicts Sayers
and her peers experienced; they also gave her a metaphor for all social relationships.

Harriet Vane and Peter Wimsey embody her central values about women and men. At the same time, they dramatize the delicate balance that maintains social harmony. As John Munting tells Elizabeth Drake, love is not enough. A man can die for a woman and still be rude to her. Mr. Puffett's earthy conclusion in *Busman's Honeymoon* gets to the point: "there's more to marriage, as they say, than four bare legs in a bed." Harriet and Peter illustrate what that more can be.

The Wimseys' and, before theirs the Muntings', marriages bind them, but do not chain them. Munting admits to Elizabeth Drake that they will backslide at times, but that candor and consideration will get them through. The Muntings and the Wimseys herald the unparalleled social revolution that Lord Peter mentions in *Gaudy Night*.

Both Harriet and Peter remain free to fulfill their separate humanities in the image of god, "something shared by male and female alike," according to Sayers. They share with each other and with God, we have noted, "the desire and the ability to make things."

Sayers recorded the following in 1938:

> "What," men have asked distractedly from the beginning of time, "what on earth do women want?" I do not know that women, *as* women, want anything in particular, but as human beings they want, my good men, exactly what you want yourselves: interesting occupation, reasonable freedom for their pleasures, and a sufficient emotional outlet. What form the occupation, the pleasures and the emotion may take, depends entirely upon the individual.

She laughed at scholars who tried to solve "what they were pleased to call the 'problem' of Queen Elizabeth" by inventing complicated explanations of her success as a ruler. "She was the tool of Burleigh, she was the tool of Leicester, she was the fool of Essex; she was diseased, she was deformed, she was a man in disguise." Sayers said that no wonder Martha and Mary were first at Jesus' cradle and last at his tomb. There had never been a man like him. He was a "prophet and teacher who never nagged at them, never flattered or coaxed or patronised; who never made arch jokes about them, never treated them either as 'The women, God help us!' or 'The ladies, God bless them!'"

In *Gaudy Night*, Harriet Vane reflects on the effect of post-World War I upon male and female students' attitudes about work. In discussing the detective novel with them, she recognizes in their enthusiasm for the genre their desire to do something definite, such as the finiteness in which a who-dunit specializes. She also recognizes that these students forget that the author manipulates fictional action to reach a definite point. Another thought from *Gaudy Night* accompanies her recognitions: "It was borne in upon Harriet that all those young men and women were starting out to hoe a hardish kind of row in a very stony ground. She felt rather sorry for them." Harriet intimates a recognition that Sayers explicitly states later: that as a habit of mind the detective pattern is inadequate.

Our Kind of Show is Dead and Done For

Towards the end of *Gaudy Night*, Lord Peter asks Harriet to accompany him on a visit to his ancestral home, Denver, to take a last look before a new civilization covers it. He predicts that it will probably be sold to a Hollywood king. As he considers the end of his family estate and all that it stood for, he remarks angrily, "Our kind of show is dead and done for."

Lord Peter tells Bunter in *Gaudy Night* "It's coming; it's here; back to the Army again, sergeant." By the end of the novel on May 20, 1935, Wimsey has been asked to return to Italy by the Foreign Office. The postwar era that saw the rise of the detective novel was about to give way to another war.

Vera Brittain's *Testament of Experience* describes the mood of those times. On May 6, 1935, England celebrated the Silver Jubilee of King George V. Brittain recalls a sign that read "FLAGS TODAY—GAS MASKS TOMOR-ROW." On January 20, 1936, the King was dead. As Lord Peter indicates in *Thrones, Dominations*, King George's death represented more than the death of a man. It was the death of a short-lived period without war. With a second war imminent, it was going to be a hardish row to hoe.

Appropriately, in Sayers's last novel when Lord Peter learns that he must return to the search for clues and the capture of a murderer, he explosively curses the old whodunit grind in a chapter entitled "Back to the Army Again." *Busman's Honeymoon* signals not only the end of Lord Peter's detecting; it also signals the beginning of a harsher time and a bleaker genre for the detective.

Sayers had begun to write detective stories with the assurance that the detective formula could find "its own proper greatness as a sonnet within the restrictions of octave and sestet." In 1936, she wistfully manifests disappointment: "We can now handle the mechanical elements of the plot with the ease of long practice; we have yet to discover the best way of combining these with a serious artistic treatment of the psychological elements, so that the intellectual and the common man can find common ground for enjoyment in the mystery novel as once they did in Greek and Elizabethan tragedy."

In *The Simple Act of Murder*, Raymond Chandler seems to suggest rightly that "what was really gnawing at Miss Sayers' mind was the slow realization that her kind of detective story was an arid formula which could not even satisfy its own implications." But perhaps we are overlooking the obvious. Sayers had said all that she needed to say by means of the detective form. The development of her craft from the merry chase of the detective puzzle to the chastening tone of her novels of manners allowed her to say what she had wanted to say about the human spirit and its relationship to the divine pattern. Two wars in three decades revealed to her the inadequacy of the detective pattern of problem-solving as a habit of mind for her age.

"Why Work?"

208510

Sayers's last two novels do not mourn the past; they suggest that there is work to be done. Like most of her detective fiction, they prepare the writer to say and the reader to hear the statements in "Why Work?" about changing one's habit of mind, particularly about the end for which one labors. In that 1949 essay, Sayers declared that war was a judgment, not an irrational catastrophe. It evolves logically from a society's misplaced confidence in a definite end in goods and payment for work.

Her aesthetics, her social views, her attitude about work have their center in a Christian belief of process. In "Towards a Christian Aesthetic," she distinguishes between the Greek and Christian views of art. The Greek, she said, never thought of art as creation; in fact, "the Greeks had not this word in their aesthetic at all. They looked on a work of art as a kind of *techné*, a manufacture. Neither, for that matter, was the word in their theology—they did not look on history as the continual act of God fulfilling itself in creation."

All work to Sayers, including the work of the artist, was the continual act of God's fulfillment in creation. She urged her society to preserve its wartime habit of valuing work for its own sake, to look at work "not as a necessary drudgery to be undergone for the purpose of making money, but as a way of life in which the nature of man should find it proper exercise and delight and so fulfill itself to the glory of God." As God is continuously fulfilling Himself in creation, so, too, is each human fulfilling himself—detective, novelist, beer manufacturer. Each must work with "a proper sense of personal responsibility" asking, Sayers professed, "What goes into the beer," not how much money can I get?

Like her fictional workers, Sayers concentrated on her job. Hers was to tell stories. To be a good storyteller according to Sayers, one first needs the ability to craft plot and to describe precise details from the world that is familiar to the audience. She explained that Dante's success as a storyteller was in his ability to focus his audience's attention "resolutely on some unde-viating purpose (which is one reason why detective stories are popular and why everybody is so much more virtuous and industrious in war than in peace)." In addition to focusing on one undeviating purpose, Dante also understood the "trick of particularity," the use of prosaic details. Details create "a vivid conviction of fact—the sort of conviction that used to lead people to address letters to 'Sherlock Holmes Esq., 221 Baker Street,' beg-ging him to investigate their problems" or to write letters to Harriet and Peter Wimsey to give them advice about child care.

Prosaic details and well-crafted plots are the technical skills that a storyteller needs to develop. But as we have noted many times in this study, Sayers's concern for her profession went beyond learning its requisite skills.

Sayers's first aim was to tell a good—meaning a well-crafted and con-sistent—story or series of stories. Her second was to create a new genre. She did not destroy the old standards of the art of detection; she synthesized their emphases on the puzzle and the rule of fair play with the social values of the novel of manners.

She also insisted that for the craft to become truth, it must develop from the artist's design as a consistent work of the imagination. An unrealistic work can be true, for truth is in the artist's integrity to her art. Sayers aimed to awaken her audience, not to lull it into a daydream. If her readers were to recognize their own faces in her art, she had first to be true to the art. "For a work of art that is not good and true *in art* is not good or true in any other respect . . . and is useless for any purpose whatsoever—even for edifica-tion—because it is a lie, and the devil is the father of all such," she wrote in the introduction of *The Man Born to Be King,* her play about the life of Jesus Christ.

Whatever imaginative universe she created would have to be consistent. If Harriet Vane was an independent, intelligent woman of honor, as she demonstrates in her trial in *Strong Poison,* she cannot succumb to Lord Peter Wimsey's unquestionable charm and energy just because he saves her life. If Peter Wimsey is to be distraught about causing a murderer's death, that behavior must relate logically to what has preceded it. Just as Wimsey finishes Harriet's poem by adhering to the form and motifs that govern its beginning, so the novelist concentrates on the direction of her art and remains true to it.

In her introduction to *The Man Born to Be King*, Sayers explained that she wrote about Christ in a manner to represent a life in a particular time and a particular place, and that if she was true to her work as a dramatist, the theology, morals, and edification would come as a result of her good work. We can say the same about her detective fiction. She represented fictional lives in a particular time in a particular place. We can also find consistency of imagination by comparing her description of one of her last works, a translation of *The Song of Roland*, with the social implications of her detective fiction.

The poem about Roland, she said, dramatizes a small central struggle that shakes the web of the larger age that surrounds it; "a private war is set within a national war, and the national war again within the world-war of Cross and Crescent." Wimsey, Bunter, local policemen, Harriet Vane, Miss Climpson, Montague Egg, armed with their codes of honor and responsibility, shake the web of the larger age of uncertainties that surround them.

The Rejoicing Universe

Finally, Sayers's detective fiction celebrates and affirms the vitality of the human spirit. She recognized an antagonist in S. S. Van Dine, who believed, in her words, "that every vestige of humanity should be ruthlessly expunged from the detective novel; but," she argued, "I am sure he is wrong. . . ." Recalling Sayers's peopled landscape, we know that he is.

Besides Peter Wimsey, Dorothy L. Sayers's name calls up those of Mervyn Bunter, Wimsey's manservant from Kent; Wimsey's close friend and brother-in-law, Charles Parker of Scotland Yard; the talkative Dowager Duchess, Wimsey's mother; his sour sister-in-law, Helen, and her husband, the doltish Gerald Wimsey, Duke of Denver; their precocious son, Pickled Gherkins; the Viscount Saint-George; Wimsey's sensible sister, Lady Mary; Freddy Arbuthnot, whose brilliance is limited to the stock market; Sir Impey Biggs, the imposing, actorlike lawyer; Mr. Murbles, the solicitor who loves caps; Miss Katherine Climpson, who turns gossip into important information; Reverend Venables, the kindly shepherd who considerately blows his horn at every dangerous turn as he tends his scattered flock; Mr. Puffet, whose broad base protrudes from beneath the chimneys as he works happily; Nobby Cranton, the timid thief; Marjorie Phelps, Harriet Vane, Elizabeth Drake, and other Sayers women; innumerable innkeepers; and the commercial traveller, Montague Egg.

Sayers's is a bustling, noisy world. We remember the conversations, such as the Dowager Duchess's early morning buckshot talk in *Whose Body?* that juxtaposes the philosophical, "Everybody Ishmaels together" with information about Lord Peter's father's dislike of business people and comments about Lady Levy's family. We remember Miss Climpson's italicized inflections; nervous Mr. Thipps's "reely" every fourth sentence; Colonel Belfridge, who punctuates his disdain of flapper votes with "Ha, Hr'rm" in *Have His Carcase*. We recall the villain Henry Weldon of the same novel, when he equates Bolsheviks, women's rights, and crystal-gazing. We remember Mrs. Cropper's voice in *Unnatural Death* as it mimics Mary Whittaker's and Miss Dawson's on the day that Miss Dawson was to have signed her will unknowingly. No one can forget Mr. Murbles's exclamations of horror at finding out about Robert Fentiman's prank on Armistice Day in *The Unpleasantness at the Bellona Club*. We recollect the intellectual energy of the conversations in *Gaudy Night*.

Readers remember the sounds and looks of Sayers's people. Besides her ability to create unusual situations that challenge us and to arrange them in unified designs that suggest more than they say, her loving skill with character portrayal leaves her people with us long after we have forgotten the intricacies of ciphers and timetables. Hers is a world of vital human beings who live in a realm of language.

"We've got to laugh or break our hearts in this damnable world," announces an older, more sombre Lord Peter in *Busman's Honeymoon*. Laughter, finally, characterizes the tone of Sayers's detective canon. As author of the Mustard Club adventures and the playful Detection Club round-robins, Sayers made a joyful noise unto the Lord. Her characters and their creator resemble the redeemed in Dante's *Divine Comedy:* ". . . for them is the song, the shouting, the celestial dance, revolving like a mill-wheel, spinning like a top . . .—for them the laughter of the rejoicing universe, for them the Divine Comedy."

We rejoice in the universe that Sayers created in her detective fiction in celebration of creation itself. In the back of an antique shop in *Gaudy Night*, Peter and Harriet sing together—"tenor and alto twined themselves in a last companionable cadence." In the most exuberant scene in *Busman's Honeymoon*, Peter and Harriet sing, "Here we sit like BIRDS in the wilderness" with Mr. Puffett, Miss Twitterton, and Mr. Goodacre.

At the New Year's Eve service in *The Nine Tailors* another community joins in song. At first, the congregation seems lost in the large church of the Fen country. Then the people begin to sing. They are joined with each other and with the divine presence evident in the cherubim and seraphim that echo the human voices from high above. "My God!" exclaims Lord Peter. His expletive appropriately expresses the majesty of the hymn, "Let everything that hath breath praise the Lord." Celebration and praise of the glory of creation characterizes Sayers's works.

Sayers discovered, by reading about Cyrus the Persian in a children's book of Greek history and later in a context that marched him "clean out of Herodotus and slap into the Bible," that literature, history, and the Bible are all of a piece. Her artistry shows similar connections. Like the dove in Genesis, Lord Peter announces God's grace after the flood. The dons in *Gaudy Night* echo women of the Renaissance. Harriet and Peter bring the sexuality of John Donne's poetry to a modern audience by using Donne's language on their honeymoon. At the end of *Gaudy Night,* they revivify an ancient ritual and language by giving them a new context of love. They replay the old tales of Cinderella and Sleeping Beauty. They recall to us the Biblical story of Adam and Eve, and Milton's image at the end of *Paradise Lost,* where Adam and Eve leave the Garden hand in hand.

Sayers's art of synthesis and consistency shows us that by being true to her work, by serving its design, the artist once again releases the powers of the old truths and of imagination.

For the artist, as for any worker, the creating is a continuous process. Sayers explained in *The Mind of the Maker* that it was no accident that her novel *Gaudy Night* and her play *The Zeal of Thy House,* written soon after it, should have the same themes. Although the former signals the end of one development, the detective novel, and the latter signals the beginning of another, Christian drama, together they illustrate the continuing creativity of Dorothy L. Sayers.

Wimsey, Roland, Dante, Jesus Christ—are connected in Sayers's mind. "At the day's end or the year's end he [the artist] may tell himself: the work is done. But he knows in his heart that it is not, and that the passion of making will seize him again the following day and drive him to construct a fresh world."

Fresh worlds abound in Sayers's detective fiction and in her subsequent essays and dramas.

NOTES

PAGE	QUOTE	SOURCE
7	"on technical points"	Dorothy L. Sayers, "Introduction" in *The Floating Admiral* (New York: Doubleday, Doran & Company, Inc., 1932), pp. 2–3.
8	"the synthetic kind"	Dorothy L. Sayers, "Trials and Sorrows of a Mystery Writer," *The Listener*, 7 (January 6, 1932), p. 26.
8/9	"happen to us"	Sayers, *Great Short Stories*, I:44.
9	"burdened in the past"	Sayers, "Introduction" in *Floating Admiral*, p. 3.
9	"nature of things?"	Dorothy L. Sayers, "The Present Status of the Mystery Story," *The London Mercury*, 23 (November 1930), pp. 51–52.
9	"of eminent scientists"	Sayers, "The Present Status," p. 47.
10	"Death in the Library"	Dorothy L. Sayers, *The Mind of the Maker* (1941; rpt. New York: Harper & Row, Publishers, 1979), p. 189.

Chapter One

PAGE	QUOTE	SOURCE
11	"swaddling clothes and their creators."	Sayers, *Great Short Stories*, III:15, quoting Galsworthy.
11	"nothing surprises us very much"	Ibid., V:15.
12	"huddled and incomprehensible summary"	Ibid. V:15.
13	"between the sea and a precipice"	Ibid., III:19.
13	"in a single surprise"	Ibid.
13	"like conventional corpses"	G. K. Chesterton, "Introduction " to *A Century of Detective Stories* (London: Hutchinson & Co., n.d.), p. ii.
13	"well-defined mannerisms"	Sayers, *Great Short Stories*, III:20.
15	"pursuit of a favorite hobby"	Dorothy L. Sayers, "Other People's Great Detectives," *Illustrated* I (April 29, 1939), p. 19.
18	"*as if* it were actually true"	Dorothy L. Sayers, *Unpopular Opinions* (London: Victor Gollancz Ltd., 1946), p. 52.

Chapter Two

PAGE	QUOTE	SOURCE
26	"parts is quite another"	Sayers, *Great Short Stories*, III:13.
26	"as well as lacunae"	Sayers, *Unpopular Opinions*, p. 54.

PAGE	QUOTE	SOURCE
26	"twist in the tail"	Dorothy L. Sayers, ed. *Tales of Detection* (London: J. M. Dent & Sons Ltd., 1936), p. xii.
26	"interplay of character"	Ibid., p. ix.
27	"the queen died"	E. M. Forster, *Aspects of the Novel* (1927; rpt. New York: Harcourt, Brace & World. Inc., 1954), p. 86.
27	"pure crossword puzzle"	Dorothy L. Sayers, "Gaudy Night," in *The Art of the Mystery Story*, ed. Howard Haycraft (1946; rpt. New York: Biblo and Tannen, 1976), p. 209.
28	"to say about life"	Ibid., p. 208.
28	"achieving artistic unity"	Sayers, *Great Short Stories*, I:37.
28	"the delicate balance"	Ibid., p. 38.
28	"level of literary achievement"	Ibid., p. 37.
28	"octave and sestet"	Sayers, "Present Status," *London Mercury*, p. 51.
28	"till he finds it"	Sayers, *Great Short Stories*, III:22.
31	"varying his surprises"	Sayers, *Great Short Stories*, I:43.
31	"provides the best entertainment"	Ibid.
39	"most interesting people"	G. K. Chesterton, *Generally Speaking* (New York: Dodd, Mead & Company, 1929), p. 6.
39	"disguised as everybody else"	Ibid.
42	"ends in wedding bells"	Sayers, *Great Short Stories*, I:44.

Chapter Three

45	"banquet for the cultured"	Sayers, "Present Status," *London Mercury*, p. 47.
45	"squeezed out of it"	Ibid. p. 51.
46	"of Lord Peter Wimsey"	A. E. Murch, *The Development of the Detective Novel* (1958; rpt. New York: Greenwood Press Publishers, 1968), p. 222.
46	"of its due time"	Sayers, "Gaudy Night," in *The Art*, p. 209.
47	"abolish, its evil"	Sayers, *Mind of the Maker*, p. 191.
49	"husband and father"	Sayers, *Great Short Stories*, I:37–38.
50	"in the last chapter"	Sayers, *Great Short Stories*, I:39.
50	"complete human being"	Sayers, "Gaudy Night" in *The Art*, p. 211.

PAGE	QUOTE	SOURCE
50	"liberating and inspiring influence"	Dorothy L. Sayers, "Introduction," in E. C. Bentley, *Trent's Last Case* (1913; rpt. New York: Harper & Row, Publishers, Inc., 1978), p. x.
51	"advice upon child-welfare"	Sayers, "Gaudy Night," in *The Art*, p. 220.

Chapter Four

55	"as it ought to be"	Sayers, "Gaudy Night," in *The Art*, p. 209.
55	"hell is within us"	Sayers, *Great Short Stories*, V:20.
57	"reading higher mathematics"	Walter R. Brooks, "Behind the Blurbs," *Outlook*, 159 (September 23, 1931), p. 123.
57	"go to his tea"	Sayers, "Trials and Sorrows," *Listener*, p. 26.
58	"won't ever start it"	Bruce Catton, "A Book a Day," syndicated in June 1, 1932, issues of small newspapers across the United States. My source was the clipping file in the Marion Wade Collection at Wheaton College.
62	"about them both"	Sayers, *Great Short Stories*, III:17.
64	"from the air"	Sayers, *Unpopular Opinions*, p. 57
64	"effectively be besieged"	Dorothy L. Sayers, "The Psychology of Advertising," *The Spectator*, 159 (November 19, 1937), p. 897.

Chapter Five

71	"in full force"	Robert Graves and Alan Hodge, *The Long Weekend: A Social History of Great Britain, 1918–1939* (New York: The Macmillan Company, 1941), p. 287.
72	"to say all my life"	Sayers, "Gaudy Night," in *The Art*, p. 213.
72	"a 'woman's novel' "	Julian Symons, *Mortal Consequences* (New York: Harper & Row, Publishers, 1972), p. 129.
79	"in a lethal chamber"	Sayers, "Gaudy Night," in *The Art*, p. 212.
82	"novel of manners"	Ibid., p. 210.

Chapter Six

89	"back to reality"	Sayers, *Unpopular Opinions*, pp. 34–35.

PAGE	QUOTE	SOURCE
89	*"personal responsibility"*	Dorothy L. Sayers, "Wimsey Papers—XI," *The Spectator*, Vol. 164 (January 26, 1940), p. 105.
90	"sense of familiarity"	Sayers, *Unpopular Opinions*, p. 40.
90	"in my own"	Ibid., p. 41.
90	"caused by wars"	Sayers, *Mind of the Maker*, p. 196.
91	"truce with evil"	Sayers, "Wimsey Papers—II, *The Spectator*, Vol. 163 (November 24, 1939), p. 736.
92	"Roland and Lancelot"	Sayers, Great Short Stories, I:13.
92	"himself to God"	Dorothy L. Sayers, "Why Work?" in *Creed or Chaos?* (New York: Harcourt, Brace and Company, 1949), p. 53.
92	"to make things"	Sayers, *Mind of the Maker*, p. 22.
92	"man's creative energy"	Ibid., p. 218.
94	"the original two"	Ibid., p. 191.
95	"unless by his Harriet"	Humphrey Carpenter, *The Inklings* (Boston: Houghton Mifflin, 1979), p. 189, quoting Tolkien.
96	"interests of domesticity"	Virginia Woolf, *A Room of One's Own* (1929; rpt. New York: Harcourt, Brace & World, Inc., 1957), p. 87.
96	"nuisance to the world"	Sayers, *Unpopular Opinions*, p. 110.
97	"male and female alike"	Sayers, *Mind of the Maker*, p. 21.
97	"entirely upon the individual"	Sayers, *Unpopular Opinions*, p. 114.
97	"of Queen Elizabeth"	Ibid., p. 111.
97	"man in disguise"	Sayers, *Unpopular Opinions*, p. 111.
97	" 'God bless them!' "	Ibid., p. 121.
98	"GAS MASKS TOMORROW"	Vera Brittain, *Testament of Experience* (New York: The Macmillan Company, 1957), p. 124.
99	"and Elizabethan tragedy"	Sayers, *Tales of Detection*, p. xiii.
99	"its own implications"	Raymond Chandler, *The Simple Art of Murder* (1939 rpt; New York: Ballantine Books, 1977), p. 14.
99	"itself in creation"	Sayers, *Unpopular Opinions*, p. 37.
99	"glory of God"	Sayers, *Creed or Chaos?* p. 46.
100	"into the beer?"	Ibid., p. 52.
100	"than in peace"	Dorothy L. Sayers, " 'And Telling You a Story,' " in *Essays Presented to Charles Williams* (London: Oxford University Press, 1947), p. 7.

PAGE	QUOTE	SOURCE
100	"investigate their problems"	Sayers, " 'And Telling You a Story,' " p. 10.
100	"father of all such"	Dorothy L. Sayers, *The Man Born to Be King* (1943, rpt; New York: Harper & Row Publishers, Inc., 1976), p. 4.
101	"Cross and Crescent"	Dorothy L. Sayers, "Introduction," *The Song of Roland* (1957, rpt; New York: Penguin Books, 1977), p. 25.
101	"he is wrong"	Sayers, "Gaudy Night," in *The Art,* p. 209.
102	"the Divine Comedy"	Dorothy L. Sayers, *Introductory Papers on Dante* (New York: Harper & Brothers Publishers, 1954), p. 174.
103	"slap into the Bible"	Sayers, *Unpopular Opinions,* p. 24.
103	"a fresh world"	Sayers, *Mind of the Maker,* p. 207.

BIBLIOGRAPHY

I. Works by Sayers

A. NOVELS

Whose Body? 1923; rpt. New York: Avon Books, 1961.
Clouds of Witness. 1927; rpt. New York: Avon Books, 1966.
Unnatural Death. 1927; rpt. New York: Avon Books, 1964.
The Unpleasantness at the Bellona Club. 1928; rpt. New York: Avon Books, 1963.
The Documents in the Case. 1930; rpt. New York: Avon Books, 1968.
Strong Poison. 1930; rpt. New York: Avon Books, 1967.
Five Red Herrings (Suspicious Characters). 1931; rpt. New York: Avon Books, 1968.
Have His Carcase. 1932; rpt. New York: Avon Books, 1968.
Murder Must Advertise. 1933; rpt. New York: Avon Books, 1967.
The Nine Tailors. 1934; rpt. New York: Harcourt, Brace & World, Inc., 1962.
Gaudy Night. 1936; rpt. New York: Avon Books, 1968.
Busman's Honeymoon: A Love Story with Detective Interruptions. 1937; rpt. New York: Avon Books, 1968.

B. SHORT STORY COLLECTIONS

Lord Peter Views the Body. 1928; rpt. New York: Avon Books, 1969.
Hangman's Holiday. 1933; rpt. New York: Avon Books, 1969.
In the Teeth of the Evidence. 1940; rpt. New York: Avon Books, 1952.
Lord Peter. Compiled, with Introduction, by James Sandoe. New York: Avon Books, 1972. (A collection of all of the Lord Peter short stories, including the final story, "Talboys.")

C. OTHER DETECTIVE FICTION
AND ESSAYS ABOUT THE ART OF DETECTION

Bentley, E. C. *Trent's Last Case.* 1931; rpt. with Introduction by Dorothy L. Sayers. New York: Harper & Row, Publishers, Inc., 1978.

111

Collins, Wilkie. *The Moonstone*. Introduction by Dorothy L. Sayers. 1944; rpt. London: J. M. Dent & Sons, Ltd., 1977.

Sayers, Dorothy L. "Detective Stories for the Screen," *Sight and Sound* 7 (Summer 1938), pp. 49–50.

————. "The Entertaining Episode of the Article in Question," in *Sleuths: Twenty-Three Great Detectives of Fiction and Their Best Stories*, ed. Kenneth Macgowan. New York: Harcourt, Brace and Company, 1931. (Contains the first biographical information about Lord Peter Wimsey.)

————. "Gaudy Night" in *The Art of the Mystery Story*, ed. Howard Haycraft. 1946; rpt. New York: Biblo and Tannen, 1976. (Originally a chapter in *Titles to Fame*, ed. Denys K. Roberts. London: Nelson, 1937.)

————. "How I Came to Invent the Character of Lord Peter," *Harcourt Brace News* I (July 15, 1936), pp. 1–2.

————. "The Murder of Julia Wallace" in *Trial and Error*, ed. Joan Kahn, Boston: Houghton Mifflin Company, 1973.

————. "Other People's Great Detectives," *Illustrated* I (April 29, 1939), pp. 18–19.

————. "The Present Status of the Mystery Story," *The London Mercury* XXIII (November 1930), pp. 47–52.

————. "Trials and Sorrows of a Mystery Writer," *The Listener*. 7 (January 6, 1932), p. 26.

"Why I Killed Peter Wimsey—by Dorothy Sayers," Interview with Val Gielgud. *Sunday Dispatch* (December 22, 1957), p. 6.

Sayers, Dorothy L., *Wilkie Collins: A Critical and Biographical Study*, ed. E. R. Gregory, Toledo, Ohio: The Friends of the University of Toledo Library, 1977.

Sayers, Dorothy L., ed. *Great Short Stories of Detection, Mystery and Horror*. 6 vols. 1952; rpt. London: Victor Gollancz Ltd., 1928 (first series), 1931 (second series), 1934 (third series).

————. *Tales of Detection*. London: J. M. Dent & Sons Ltd., 1936.

Sayers, Dorothy L., *et al. Ask a Policeman*. New York: William Morrow & Company, 1933.

————. *Double Death: A Murder Story*. London: Victor Gollancz Ltd., 1939.

————. *The Floating Admiral*. Garden City, N.Y.: Doubleday, Doran & Company, Inc., 1932.

Sayers, Dorothy L., and M. St. Clare Byrne. "Busman's Honeymoon: A Detective Comedy in Three Acts" in *Famous Plays of 1937*. London: Victor Gollancz Ltd., 1937.

D. ON MATTERS OTHER THAN DETECTION

"'. . . And Telling You a Story': A Note on *The Divine Comedy*," in *Essays Presented to Charles Williams*. London: Oxford University Press,. 1947.

Are Women Human? Introduction by Mary McDermott Shideler. Grand Rapids: William B. Eerdmans Publishing Co., 1971. (Reprinted from *Unpopular Opinions*.)

The Comedy of Dante Alighieri the Florentine. (Translation and Introduction by Sayers.) Rpt. Middlesex, Eng.: Penguin Books, 1977. *Hell (L'Inferno)* was first published in 1949; *Purgatory (Il Purgatorio)*, in 1955; *Paradise (Il Paradiso)*, in 1962. (Barbara Reynolds completed the latter after Sayers's death in 1957.)

Creed or Chaos? New York: Harcourt, Brace and Company, 1949.

Further Papers on Dante. New York: Harper & Brothers, 1957.

"Ink of Poppies," *The Spectator*, no. 5681 (May 14, 1937), pp. 897–98.

Introductory Papers on Dante. New York: Harper & Brothers 1954.

The Man Born to Be King. 1943; rpt. Grand Rapids, Mich.: William B. Eerdmans Publishing Co., 1976.

The Mind of the Maker. 1941; rpt. New York: Harper & Row, Publishers, 1979.

OP. I. Oxford: B. H. Blackwell, 1916. (This small collection includes Sayers's poems "Going-down Play" and "Last Morning in Oxford.")

"The Psychology of Advertising," *The Spectator*, no. 5708 (November 19, 1937), pp. 896–98.

The Song of Roland. (Translation and introduction by Sayers.) 1957; rpt. New York: Penguin Books, 1977.

Preface to *The Surprise* by G. K. Chesterton. London: Sheed and Ward, 1952.

Unpopular Opinions. London: Victor Gollancz Ltd., 1946. "Wimsey Papers I–XI," in *The Spectator*, vols. 163, 164 (November 1939–January 1940).

"Would You Like to be 21 Again?—I Wouldn't," *The Daily Express*, no. 11461 (February 9, 1937), p. 10.

The Zeal of Thy House. Acting Edition for the Friends of Canterbury Cathedral. Canterbury, Eng.: H. J. Goulden, Limited, 1937. Reprinted with permission of Sayers and Victor Gollancz, Ltd.

II. Works about Sayers

Blake, Nicholas. "Gaudeamus Igitur," *The Spectator*, vol. 155 (November 15, 1935), p. 828.

Brittain, Vera. *The Women at Oxford.* London: George G. Harrap & Co. Ltd., 1960. (Includes several pages of biographical information about Sayers.)

Brooks, Walter R. "Behind the Blurbs," *Outlook* 159 (September 23, 1931), p. 121. (Review of *Five Red Herrings.)*

Catton, Bruce. "A Book a Day." Syndicated in several newspapers in June 1932. (Wheaton College, Marion E. Wade Collection clipping file: *Gazette*, Gastonia, N.C.: *Telegraph-Herald*, Dubuque, Idaho; *News*, Frederick, Md.; *Post-Tribune*, Gary, Ind.)

Cawelti, John G. *Adventure, Mystery, and Romance.* Chicago: University of Chicago Press, 1976. (Includes discussion of *The Nine Tailors*.)

Dale, Alzina Stone. "Fossils in Cloud-Cuckoo Land," *The Sayers Review*, Vol. 3 (December 1978), pp. 1–13.

――――. *Maker and Craftsman: The Story of Dorothy L. Sayers*. Grand Rapids, Mich.: William B. Eerdmans Publishing Co., 1978.

Frankenburg, Charis U. *Not Old, Madam, Vintage*, Lavenham and Suffolk, Eng.: Galaxy Press, 1975. (Includes recollections of Sayers at Oxford in the early 1900s.)

Hamilton, Edith. "Gaudeamus Igitur," *Saturday Review of Literature*, Vol. 13 (February 22, 1936), p. 6. (Review of *Gaudy Night*.)

Heilbrun, Carolyn. "Sayers, Lord Peter and God," *American Scholar*, Vol. 37 (Spring 1968), pp. 324–34. (Reprinted in *Lord Peter*, compiled by James Sandoe.)

Hitchman, Janet. *Such a Strange Lady*. New York: Avon Books, 1976.

Hone, Ralph E. *Dorothy L. Sayers: A Literary Biography*. Kent, Ohio: Kent State University Press, 1979.

Lee, G. A., and Alzina Stone Dale. "The Wimsey Saga," *The Sayers Review*, Vol. 3 (December 1978), pp. 14–20.

McCarthy, Mary. "Highbrow Shockers," *The Nation*, Vol. 142 (April 8, 1936), pp. 458–59. (Review of *Gaudy Night*.)

Scott-Giles, C. W. *The Wimsey Family*. New York: Harper & Row, Publishers, 1977.

III. General Essays on Detective Fiction

Auden, W. H. "The Guilty Vicarage," *The Dyer's Hand and Other Essays*. London: Faber and Faber, 1962. (Describes Peter Wimsey as a priggish superman.)

Bentley, E. C., ed. *The Second Century of Detective Stories*. London: Hutchinson & Co., n.d.

――――. *Those Days*. London: Constable & Co., Ltd., 1940. (Chapter IX tells the story of *Trent's Last Case*.)

Chandler, Raymond. *The Simple Art of Murder*. 1939; rpt. New York: Ballantine Books Edition, 1977.

Chesterton, G. K., ed. *A Century of Detective Stories*. London: Hutchinson & Co., n.d.

――――. "Detective Story Writers," *Come to Think of It*. New York: Dodd, Mead & Company, 1931.

――――. "A Defence of Detective Stories," *The Defendant*. London: J. M. Dent & Sons, Ltd., 1901.

――――. "Detective Stories," *G.K.C. as M.C.: Being a Collection of Thirty-Seven Introductions*. Selected and edited by J. P. de Fonseka. London: Methuen & Co. Ltd., 1929.

――――. "On Detective Novels," *Generally Speaking*. New York: Dodd, Mead & Company, 1929.

Haycraft, Howard, ed. *The Art of the Mystery Story: A Collection of Critical Essays.* 1946; rpt. New York: Biblo and Tannen, 1976.

———. *Fourteen Great Detective Stories.* Revised edition. New York: Modern Library, 1949.

———. *Murder for Pleasure: The Life and Times of the Detective Story.* New York: D. Appleton-Century Company, 1941.

McCarthy, Mary. "Murder and Karl Marx," *The Nation,* Vol. 42 (March 25, 1936), pp. 381–83.

McLuhan, Herbert Marshall. "Footprints in the Sands of Crime," *Sewanee Review,* Vol. 54 (Autumn 1946), pp. 617–34.

Murch, A. E. *The Development of the Detective Novel.* 1958; rpt. New York: Greenwood Press, Publishers, 1968.

Rhode, John, ed. *Detection Medley.* London: Hutchinson & Co. Ltd., 1939. (Rhode discusses the Detection Club in his Foreword. This anthology contains Sayers's "Striding Folly" and "The Haunted Policeman.")

Symons, Julian. *Mortal Consequences.* New York: Harper & Row, Publishers, 1972.

Symons, Julian, ed. *Verdict of Thirteen: A Detection Club Anthology.* New York: Harper & Row, Publishers, 1978.

"Too Many Corpses in Detective Fiction," *The Literary Digest,* Vol. 112 (February 27, 1932), p. 18. (Quotes J. B. Priestley on popular fiction.)

Wilson, Edmund. "'Mr. Holmes, They Were the Footprints of a Gigantic Hound,'" *Classics and Commercials.* New York: Farrar, Straus and Company, 1950. (This collection includes "Who Cares Who Killed Roger Ackroyd?" in which Wilson contests those who say that Dorothy Sayers writes well, and "Why Do People Read Detective Stories?")

Winn, Dilys, ed. *Murder Ink: The Mystery Reader's Companion.* New York: Workman Publishing Co., Inc., 1977.

IV. Miscellaneous Works Consulted

A. ABOUT BRITISH SOCIAL AND CULTURAL HISTORY

Brittain, Vera. *Testament of Experience: An Autobiographical Story of the Years 1925–1950.* New York: The Macmillan Company, 1957.

———. *Testament of Youth: An Autobiographical Study of the Years 1900–1925.* London: Victor Gollancz Ltd., 1933.

Fussell, Paul. *The Great War and Modern Memory.* London: Oxford University Press, 1975.

Graves, Robert, and Alan Hodge. *The Long Week-End: A Social History of Great Britain 1918–1939.* New York: The Macmillan Company, 1941.

Pound, Reginald. *Mirror of the Century: The Strand Magazine, 1891–1950.* New York: A. S. Barnes and Co., 1966.

B. ABOUT CHANGE RINGING

"The Changing of the Bells," *Yankee* (December 1978), 82–85, 177–78, 181.

An Elementary Handbook for Beginners in the Art of Change-Ringing. Issued under
   the authority of the Central Council of Church Bell Ringers. 1976. (Provided by
   the Marion E. Wade Collection.)

Martin, Ann G. "Change Ringing," *The Living Church*, Vol. 177 (December 3,
   1978), pp. 12–19.

Wilson, Wilfred G. *Change Ringing.* Available from North American Guild Book
   Service. n.d. (Also provided by the Marion E. Wade Collection.)

C. ABOUT CRICKET

The Oxford Companion to Sports and Games. Ed. James Arlott. London: Oxford University Press, 1975. (Useful for American readers of *Murder Must Advertise*.)

D. OTHER WORKS CONSULTED

Black, Henry Campbell. *Black's Law Dictionary.* Revised Fourth Edition. St. Paul,
   Minn.: West Publishing Co., 1968

Carpenter, Humphrey. *The Inklings: C. S. Lewis, J. R. R. Tolkein, Charles Williams,
   and Their Friends.* Boston: Houghton Mifflin Company, 1979.

Foster, E. M. *Aspects of the Novel.* 1927; rpt. New York: Harcourt, Brace, & World,
   Inc., 1954.

Gregory, E. R., ed. *Wilkie Collins: A Critical and Biographical Study.* Toledo, Ohio:
   The Friends of the University of Toledo Libraries, 1977.

Poe, Edgar Allan. *The Complete Works of Edgar Allan Poe*, 17 vols. Ed. James A.
   Harrison. New York: Thomas Y. Crowell & Company, 1902.

Russell, Leonard, ed. *Parody Party.* 1936; rpt. Port Washington, N.Y.: Kennikat
   Press, 1970. (Includes E. C. Bentley's parody of *Gaudy Night*, "Greedy Night,"
   which is reprinted in Sandoe's compilation, *Lord Peter.*

————. *Writing for the Press.* London: A. & C. Black, Ltd., 1935.

Snow, C. P. *The Search.* 1934; rpt. and revised London: Macmillan & Co., Ltd.,
   1958.

Woolf, Virginia. *A Room of One's Own.* 1929; rpt. New York: Harcourt, Brace &
   World, Inc., 1957.

E. BIBLIOGRAPHIES

Gilbert, Coleen B. *Bibliography of the Works of Dorothy L. Sayers.* Hamden, Conn.:
   Archon Books, 1978. (Anyone who wants to research Sayers's works should have
   this excellent guide.)

Hannay, Margaret P., ed. *As Her Wimsey Took Her: Critical Essays on the Work of Dorothy L. Sayers*. Kent, Ohio: The Kent State University Press, 1979. (See especially "Dorothy L. Sayers's Manuscripts and Letters in Public Collections in the United States," by Joe R. Christopher, *et al*. The description of the Wheaton manuscripts will enlighten readers about Sayers's unpublished manuscripts.

Harmon, Robert B., and Margaret A. Burger. *An Annotated Guide to the Works of Dorothy L. Sayers*. New York: Garland Publishing Inc., 1977.

INDEX

119